How To Start a Successful AirBNB Business

How To Start a Successful AirBNB Business

Kelly Higgins

Contents

Introduction

The Mindset You Need To Embrace Starting Today

Unleash Your Full Business Potential

Three Guys, Three Air Mattresses And A Two Word Headline

Is Airbnb Hosting Right For You

Choosing An Airbnb Business Structure

How to Conduct Airbnb Market Research Like A Seasoned Pro

TREEHOUSE AIRBNB STORY

How to Create House Rules for Your Airbnb Listing

How to Create the Perfect Airbnb House Manual

Airbnb Business Expenses: A Guide to What You Can Deduct

The Top 10 Airbnb Hosting Mistakes to Avoid

5 Tips For Taking Perfect Airbnb Photos

Airbnb Listing Tips: How to Create the Perfect Listing That Will Stand Out From the Crowd

5 Powerful Ways to Boost Your Airbnb Search Rankings

How to guarantee 5 star Airbnb reviews

Automating Your Airbnb Business

More Automation Equals More Bookings

Automate Your Airbnb Pricing

Get Rid of the Keys: How to Automate Your Airbnb Check-In

The Complete Guide to Automating Your Airbnb Business

Airbnb hosting in 2023: the pros, the cons, and everything in between

Your New Airbnb Hosting Mindset

Introduction

I envy you. No seriously, really, I do.

I only *wish* this book had been around when I was looking to get in on the Airbnb craze so many years ago.

I think about the hundreds of hours, the thousands of dollars and the God knows how many hairs I tore out of my head I would have saved had I had my hands on this book years ago. Good news is that you do not have to suffer like I did.

Finally having finished this, I want only *one* thing,

I want you to succeed as an Airbnb host.

I want you to take all of the encouragement and proven strategies and insights in this book and put them into action because I am more convinced than ever that running an Airbnb hosting business with even one room will become contagious.

In this book, you will learn:

- The Mindset You Need For Airbnb
- How To Unleash Your Full Business Potential
- How Three Guys, Three Air Mattresses And A Two Word Headline Changed The World
- How To Choose The Right Airbnb Business Structure
- How To Conduct Airbnb Market Research
- How To Create House Rules For Your Airbnb Listing
- How To Create The Perfect Airbnb House Manual

- How To Really Handle Airbnb Business Expenses
- How To Avoid The Top Hosting Mistakes
- How To Crush It Taking Airbnb Photos
- How To Write The Perfect Listing
- How To Automate Your Airbnb Business
- Airbnb Hosting In 2023: The Pros, Cons, & Everything In Between
- How To Boost Your Airbnb Search Rankings
- How To Guarantee 5 Star Airbnb Reviews
- Your Brand Spanking New Airbnb Mindset

...and so much more.

Okay. reality check and a big one...

Do nothing with the information I have fought to find and guess what happens.

Not a thing.

So humor me. Go through this book page by jam-packed page and then create your new Airbnb hosting business.

Do that for me.

Do that for you.

Kelly Higgins

If you find value in this book, I ask only that you leave a review as that is how I grow my business.

Take just a few minutes of your time and leave me an honest review, the same way you will want guests to leave you their reviews.

Thank you!

The Mindset You Need To Embrace Starting Today

Do you have a great idea for a business but are unsure how to get started?

Entrepreneurship can be daunting, especially when you're first starting out. But the truth is, with the right mindset and a bit of hard work, anyone can turn their vision into a successful venture. In this book, we'll discuss the mindset you need to start your own business, including tips on how to think like an entrepreneur.

Read on to find out how to take the first steps to launching your own business!

Define what success looks like for you

Okay, let's dive way in here. When starting a business, it's essential to have a clear understanding of what success looks like to you. For some entrepreneurs, success may be measured by the amount of money they earn; for others, it may be about making a positive impact in the community or being able to set their own hours. Taking the time to define success for yourself is an important part of setting yourself up for success.

Begin by asking yourself why you are starting your business. What are your goals and ambitions?

Do you want to make a certain amount of money? Have a certain lifestyle? Help others? Think through what it would look like to achieve those goals and define what success looks like for you. This will help you to stay focused and motivated as you work towards your vision.

The important thing to remember is that success looks different for everyone. Don't feel like you have to measure success in monetary terms if that's not what you truly want. Absolutely focus on what you value and think about how you can create a business that will bring you closer to achieving your goals.

One step in front of the other starting righty about now! And once you have defined your idea of success, write it down somewhere and use it as motivation as you continue on your entrepreneurial journey.

Believe in yourself

Let's be brutally honest. It may sound cliché, but if you want to be successful in business, you need to believe in yourself. A zillion percent.

It's important to understand that you are capable of achieving success and not be overwhelmed by any challenges that come your way. Believing in yourself is the key to making it through the difficult times and taking the necessary steps to make your business a success.

Imagine yourself already successful/ This is one of the most powerful things any 7 figure sports psychologist tells his best athlete.

To stay motivated, create a list of accomplishments and successes. This will help you to stay focused on your goals and remind you why you chose to become an entrepreneur.

Starting immediately, you need to think of yourself as the leader of your business, and speak positively about yourself and what you are doing. Always.

Having a supportive network can also help you to maintain your belief in yourself. Connecting with like-minded entrepreneurs and mentors who have been successful in their own right can help to provide you with guidance, advice and motivation. Surround yourself with success and guess which ways your mind starts to work.

Successful business people will be able to give you insight into what has worked for them and offer encouragement throughout the journey.

Be coachable

This one is such a wonderful catch-22. So let this wash over you.

One of the most important mindsets you need to possess if you want to start your own business is to be coachable. It's essential to be open to advice and feedback from those around you. You might think that a blinding commitment to your own thoughts and goals and dreams is the answer.

It's not. And the biggest, most successful people like Elon and Jeff constantly surround themselves with people smarter than them.

Surround yourself with people who can help guide and mentor you, such as mentors in the industry or experienced entrepreneurs. Talk to them endless and learn from their experiences. Ask for help when needed, and take advantage of any resources they can offer. The value you will gain here is not measurable.

It's also important to not just listen to other people's advice but to also act on it. Be willing to try new things and make changes when necessary. Coachability is so key to this entire process you right now have no idea. Yet.

Don't be afraid to pivot or adjust your business plan as you learn more about the industry and your target market. Your new Airbnb business.

The more willing you are to take advice from those around you, the faster you'll be able to make progress in your business journey. And as you will discover in this book there are more than enough people like that in groups that will do that for and with you.

Don't give up

Sounds so simple…but the fact of the matter is that less than 10% of people starting an Airbnb business will never put in all of the time and energy needed. If it was so easy to make 6 or 7 figures on Airbnb, why isn't everyone doing it?

'Cause they give up.

'Cause hard work takes work.

No matter how difficult it may seem, never give up on your dreams. Starting a business is not easy and you will face obstacles along the way. Don't ever, ever let those obstacles stand in the way of your success. Use those obstacles as pure motivation to keep going and get better.

Goes without saying, but real success doesn't happen overnight and it requires a ton of hard work and dedication. If you find yourself stuck in a rut, take a step back, reevaluate your strategy, and find new ways to move forward.

It's also important to maintain a positive attitude. It's easy to become frustrated and lose sight of your goals when things don't go as planned. Think of how easy it would be to toss it all in and start binging on Netflix again and in the process never reaching those goals you hold so dear.

Let me be very clear about one thing if it is not seeping through already: I Want Your Success. Period. Again, I put this book together from start to finish because I Want Your Success.

Always remember that you have the power to turn any negative situation into a positive one.

History keeps showing everyone that by keeping your head up and your eyes on the prize, you can break through any obstacle in your way and make progress towards achieving your goals.

Do not EVER up no matter what stands in your way. Ever.

Take risks

Ah, here come both the meat and the potatoes. It is beyond important that you fully understand that taking risks is a major part of being an entrepreneur. This is you removing limitations and you suddenly phishing yourself to do something new and exciting and potentially wildly profitable at scale. The only way to achieve this level of success is to take calculated risks, as they are necessary to grow and progress. Please take the time to read that last sentence as many times as you need to.

Hey, no one's talking about going all nutty. It's vitally important to keep in mind that while risks are important, they need to be calculated. Every decision you make should be based on research, experience, and data.

Failures and mistakes are going to happen, they must be addressed and they are a huge part of the process. Einstein knew all about the thousand failures he needed before he got to the good stuff. Embrace the missteps as pure learning.

Embrace change

Nope, its not easy, but you're about to do it. Guaranteed.

One of the most important things to remember when starting a business is that change is also one of the most inevitable. No matter how successful your business is today, you will still have to embrace change in order to stay ahead of the competition and remain profitable.

Need proof? Go ask Yahoo how they're doing.

As a business owner, and especially as an Airbnb host, you must be flexible and willing to make changes that will benefit you both in the short and long term. Change can come from internal sources such as staff changes, customer feedback, technological advances, or other external influences. To stay on top of the game, you must be able to quickly adapt to new situations and make informed decisions. (PS. Google changes its mainframe algorithm 600 times or more per year. Telling, isn't it?)

Embracing change can be challenging but it's an essential part of running a successful business.

Be open to new ideas, stay up to date on industry trends, and don't be afraid to take risks. With the right mindset and a willingness to adapt, you can set yourself up for success.

Persevere

I love this one.

One of the most important traits an entrepreneur must have is perseverance. The business world can be unpredictable, and while we all know it, success doesn't happen overnight. Hell, most times it never happens at all if you want brutal honesty here.

You one hundred and ninety percent need to be willing to put in the time and effort to build something lasting and successful. This means you need to be resilient and patient, never giving up no matter how hard it gets.

I saw a great motivational guy recently on YouTube and he had one message that he beat into his followers like clockwork. You may not be smarter than your competitors, but you can always outwork them. Always.

Great message.

Don't let setbacks stop you—acknowledge them and move on. Take risks, but also make sure you're prepared for whatever may come your way.

Oh, a word about you for a moment. Don't forget to take damn good care of yourself as you embark on this journey—take breaks when needed and don't be afraid to ask for help. Some of the top 8 figure internet marketers have a rule of going 2 hours on and then one half hour off…no matter what. That's because that shortened time forces you to work smarter in it.

It should go without saying that having a good support system is essential for staying motivated and inspired to keep going when times are tough. Just know that not everyone one in the family and friends' basket will think this is a good idea.

Persevere and prove them wrong. How simple was that?

Be passionate

True, blinding passion is an essential element of success when it comes to starting a business. Sure it's one thing to have the knowledge and skills to run a successful business, but if you don't have a genuine passion for what you're doing, it ain't happening. Sorry half-full cupfolks. It just doesn't.

Never stop being passionate about the products or services you offer, the customers you serve, and the mission you are striving to achieve in terms of being one of the best hosts ever no matter how big or small your properties are.

Be prepared to work hard

Ah, yes, the gorilla in the room...pun certainly intended.

One of the key mindsets needed as of you reading this sentence is that a successful business is the end result of hard work. End of story. Mic drop moment.

Starting a business requires dedication, long hours and a lot of hard work. You need to be ready to make sacrifices and put in the extra effort to reach your goals.

You need to plan out your goals and timeline and then put in the time and energy to achieve them and also to imagine that they are simply waiting for you as the result of all of that work.

Take risks, try new things. Invite yourself into the unknown. Sure, you're going to hit setbacks along the way. Deal with them grow from them...and outwork everyone.

Be organized

It's not blah, blah blah by any stretch. You need to really get the fact that business organization is essential for any successful business.

Have a pre-written plan for how you are going to manage the various tasks associated with running your own hosting business. Create a schedule and stick to it; make sure you understand when you need to be working on specific tasks and when you need to take breaks. Take the time to develop systems and processes that will help you stay organized, including budgeting, task management, and goal setting.

I myself was a nightmare at organization until I finally realized that either I had to get there, or had to bring in someone who could for me. There were no other options. My results since that moment have been transformative.

Unleash Your Full Business Potential

Not a single one of us does not know the feeling of being caught inside a rut, unsure of how to make the next big move in your business?

Happens to everyone, a lot.

Real success in business, of course, is a challenge, but with the right pre-written in a book strategy, it is possible to unlock your ultimate business potential. In this chapter, I drop some key tips and strategies to help you take your business to the next level. Cause that's going to happen.

Determine your purpose

When it comes to unlocking your ultimate business potential, the first step is to determine your true purpose. So that means it is time for a heavy dose of self honesty.

What do you want to achieve with your hosting business? Are you looking to make a profit, to help people, or to fulfill a creative passion?

It's critical to have a clear, unfiltered, and brutally honest understanding of why you are doing what you're doing before setting out on the Airbnb journey.

Time to create your mission statement.

Your deeply honest mission statement should be a concise overview of your goals and values. Consider it to be a compass that will endlessly guide you in the right direction when you're feeling overwhelmed or unfocused. Because overwhelmed and unfocused will happen. But perhaps less so having read this book/

Taking the time to determine your true motivation and purpose at the start of your journey is a tremendously important first step towards unlocking your ultimate hosting business potential.

However, it is just as crucial that you also understand the skills and resources you need for that success. You know what is in your talent toolbox that you can and will bring to the table. You now need to be willing to again be honest with the skills you still need to develop.

If you're getting a sense that I believe that internal honesty is a massive factor in your ultimate success then give yourself a cookie.

To me, it is the most important ones of all. Honesty at the highest level with yourself will move you towards the right thing to do for everyone each and every step of the hosting way.

Also it should go without saying out loud that having access to the right resources—including financial capital, technological resources, or mentorship—are key to reaching your objectives.

And since we've made that decision to go heavy with the self honesty at all costs...go right ahead and recognize that success does not and will not happen overnight.

Create a plan

Creating a pre-written out plan to reach your ultimate business potential is the foundation for success. And putting it somewhere that you can see it every day is something you have to do.

In your own handwriting, your plan needs to be detailed, yet flexible and realistic. It should take into account where you are now and where you want to go in the future. And not just monetarily.

Start by analyzing your current situation: What do you have to work with? What resources do you have available to you? What skills and knowledge do you possess? Then, define your goals. Think about both short-term and long-term objectives, and consider how they can be measured.

Cool, you've identified your goals, time to create your handwritten action plan. List out all the steps needed to reach each goal, including those that may need to be taken first, such as research or developing resources. When possible, break down the plan into manageable tasks that can be accomplished within a certain time frame. Then, assign dates for completion of each task.

Finally, set aside time for regularly evaluating and adjusting your plan.

Did I mention that you will find all of those topics in order specifically discussed in this book?

Did I mention that?

Constantly refine your plan. Then hang it back up where you can see it again (there's a reason for that, trust me.). Assess how well you're staying on track and make adjustments as needed. Leave the fluff language far behind and be harsh on how you are actually doing. Do that for yourself. Do that to hold yourself accountable.

It's way too early for this, but allow yourself to think about identifying areas where you might need additional support and consider hiring freelancers or contractors who have expertise in particular areas.

Never, ever stop staying ultra motivated and determined!

I wrote this book so that never happens, now you have to do your part,

Set realistic goals

Setting realistic goals is essential to reaching your ultimate business potential. Small steps always doing the next right thing is how this works.

Sure, it's easy to get carried away with grandiose ambitions, but it is important to create achievable objectives every day that you force yourself to hit.

Routine will become your friend here.

Start by defining the scope of your project and what you want to accomplish in a specific time period. Break down your goals into smaller, manageable chunks and prioritize the most important ones.

Key to all of this is that when setting goals, you need to make sure they are Specific, Measurable, Achievable, Relevant and Timely (SMART). Setting SMART goals allows you to have a clear understanding of what needs to be done, how it should be done, and when it should be completed.

Finally, and this is a big one. Remember to reward yourself when you reach a goal or milestone. Celebrating small successes along the way drives a person like nothing else.

Feed on that.

Leverage feedback from your visitors to stay ahead of trends and make necessary changes quickly. Treat each and every one of these insights and making them all part of your new Airbnb life will guarantee that you completely distance yourself from your so called competition.

Outwork and outplan everyone. And never stop.

Quick note here: as much as you can take advantage of workshops, courses, and mentorship opportunities that can expand your knowledge base and improve your skillset. Visit sites like Udemy for courses in your niche and devour them.

Stay more informed than anyone and then outwork and overdeliver.

Anyone picking up on a theme here?

Take action

The final step in realizing your ultimate business potential is you taking action.

Taking action involves more than just setting goals and making plans, it means putting in hard work necessary to make your hosting and financial dreams a reality.

Hold the phone/ That gives me a thought.

When you are done with this chapter go get more coffee and open your hosting account on Airbnb and make this 100% real. Put yourself on the clock and on the grid.

Don't yes me on this.

Go do it.

Now.

When you are up and running focus on those hosting tasks that are most important. Important here to note that as you complete each task, reward yourself with something that will motivate you to keep going. And if a cookie is the thing, a cookie is the thing.

Always and for the rest of time, reflect on how far you have come and celebrate the milestones you reach as you move closer towards achieving your ultimate business potential.

Above all, it is so so so important for you to remember that you reaching your ultimate Airbnb business potential is a journey and one that requires dedication, patience, and perseverance.

As of today and for every day forward you are not allowed to become discouraged if you encounter obstacles or challenges along the way. You are instructed by me right here to learn from your mistakes and use them as a stepping stone to success. Because that is all about to happen.

Evaluate and adjust

Once you start to make daily achievements, which will be inevitable now, it's important to evaluate yourself and your achievements with that new honesty you now have with yourself.

That honesty that is at a level you never may have had with yourself before.

To begin evaluating, take a look at your data. This could be anything from sales numbers and customer feedback to website traffic and conversion rates. Track the changes over time and analyze the results to determine what is working and what isn't. Some of the super hosts will tell you in no uncertain terms that it is far better to know what you are bad at rather than what your strengths are.

Leave your ego aside and get real with what needs to be done better by you.

Constantly ask yourself "What went wrong?", "What did I do well?", "What could I have done differently"?

Once you have identified the areas in your game that need immediate improvement, create a handwritten plan to adjust your strategy accordingly. And the one you can see in your everyday life.

Evaluating and adjusting your business plan will help you reach your ultimate business potential and ensure that you continue to stay ahead of the competition.

Not a single successful Airbnb host has left out the pressing need to create an entire online presence. Don't just consider starting a website or utilizing social media platforms to share valuable content about your products or services…do it and do it every day.

You're Going To Crush It On Airbnb Here's How I Know

Three Guys, Three Air Mattresses And A Two Word Headline

Story # 1

In 2008, Airbnb was born from a simple idea: provide a platform for people to rent out their homes to travelers.

Over the next decade, this concept would revolutionize the travel and hospitality industry, making Airbnb one of the most successful companies in the world.

In 2008, three friends, Brian Chesky, Joe Gebbia, and Nathan Blecharczyk, found themselves in San Francisco with no jobs and not enough money to pay the rent. With a unique idea, the trio decided to turn their entrepreneurial dreams into reality. They set up an online platform to list and book accommodations from hosts.

Thus, Airbnb was born.

Chesky and Gebbia bought three airbeds and set up a basic website to offer their guests the opportunity to stay in their loft apartment. The website was designed to be simple, yet efficient – much like their slogan "Live there".

The trio took a huge risk by leaving their jobs and investing all their energy into the business venture. They were able to make ends meet in the beginning by working various odd jobs while they built their business model. After testing it out with real people, they decided to move forward and build a larger network of hosts.

Then, with the help of some angel investors, they managed to get enough capital to develop a more comprehensive platform.

By 2009, the website had over 2,500 listings in 16 cities across the US. This early success gave them further confidence and they continued developing the platform. Throughout 2010 and 2011, they continued expanding Airbnb's reach to include even more cities.

The success of Airbnb proved that there was an untapped potential in sharing economy and it continues to be an inspiration for many budding entrepreneurs around the world. In 2012, Airbnb secured its first major round of funding and since then has gone on to become one of the most valuable private companies in the world.

Today, it operates in 191 countries and has over 6 million listings worldwide. It also offers users additional services such as experiences and travel activities.

The success story of Airbnb is a testament to the power of ambition, hard work and innovation and shows that great things can happen when you put your mind to it.

The first steps

In 2007, Joe Gebbia and Brian Chesky, two friends with a shared vision, decided to rent out airbeds in their San Francisco loft. They quickly realized that the travel industry was expensive and lacked personalization. With this in mind, they developed an online marketplace where people could book unique accommodations around the world.

They began by attending events like South by Southwest to drum up interest and create a buzz. They then set up a simple website and leveraged Craiglist as a way to advertise their service. From there, they created user-friendly tools that made it easy for travelers to find and book accommodations on the site.

In addition to promoting their service, Gebbia and Chesky also worked hard to build trust with their users. For example, they implemented a user review system so that customers could read about past experiences. They also provided 24/7 customer support so that anyone who had an issue could get help immediately.

Within the first few months, their company had grown to over 10,000 users and they started to receive press attention. It was clear that they had tapped into something special and their business was taking off.

Facing challenges

When Airbnb first started, the founders had no idea how to run a business, let alone an online marketplace. They had limited resources and no prior experience in starting a company, so there were certainly a lot of challenges ahead.

One of the first major issues was how to generate revenue. They needed to find a way to charge for their services without scaring off potential customers. To solve this issue, they decided to take a commission from each reservation booked through the platform. This allowed them to make money while still providing an affordable service.

The second challenge was getting people to use the platform. In the early days, the website was not very user-friendly or intuitive, making it difficult for people to find listings or book stays. To combat this, the founders spent a great deal of time and energy improving the design and usability of the site.

Finally, Airbnb had to overcome the mistrust that potential guests had about staying with strangers in an unfamiliar city. To tackle this issue, the founders developed a verification system for hosts and guests that included background checks, reviews, and ratings.

This helped to make guests feel more comfortable with the platform and encouraged more people to try out Airbnb. It also created a sense of accountability among users, which helped to build trust in the community. As more and more people began using the platform, word spread and its popularity began to grow.

Soon enough, Airbnb was able to expand into other cities around the world, allowing even more people to enjoy its services.

Since then, the company has grown exponentially, and is now considered one of the most successful start-ups ever.

Today, Airbnb offers its services in over 220 countries and regions across the world and is used by millions of travelers every day. It is truly an inspiring story of what can be accomplished with hard work and dedication.

Overcoming obstacles

The early days of Airbnb were filled with obstacles, and there was no guarantee that the founders would be successful. In order to get the business off the ground, they had to overcome a number of challenges. One of the biggest was convincing people to trust strangers enough to stay in their homes.

In order to make this happen, the team had to focus on creating trust. They established their safety policies, developed a secure payment system, and created a review system so guests could provide feedback on their experience. This gave potential guests peace of mind and encouraged them to give Airbnb a try.

Additionally, the founders faced legal battles in various cities due to the fact that they were operating outside of existing regulations. They worked hard to find a way to comply with local laws while still offering an innovative and disruptive service. This process was long and difficult, but it paid off as

Airbnb was eventually able to enter new markets without issue.

Finally, Airbnb faced stiff competition from established hotels and rental companies. The team responded by focusing on creating a superior customer experience. They listened to their users, addressed their needs, and worked to ensure that their platform was easy to use and enjoyable for everyone involved.

By tackling these challenges head on and staying focused on providing an exceptional service, Airbnb was able to overcome its obstacles and become a successful business. Over time, the platform grew steadily and began to attract more customers.

Today, Airbnb is used by millions of people around the world who rely on it to book unique accommodation experiences. It has also spawned an entirely new industry - home sharing - that has revolutionized the hospitality industry.

This success story is proof that with a bit of determination and creative problem-solving skills, anything is possible. Airbnb's story serves as an inspiration for budding entrepreneurs everywhere who are looking to make their dreams come true. Through hard work and perseverance, even seemingly impossible goals can be achieved if you put your mind to it.

Becoming a success story

Airbnb's story of success is one that continues to inspire and motivate entrepreneurs today. After their first few months of trying out their new concept, they started to see some success, and they quickly built up momentum. They started to get more attention from the press and potential investors, and in 2008, they were able to raise a round of funding.

Since then, Airbnb has grown exponentially. It now operates in more than 220 countries and regions, and is estimated to be worth over $30 billion. The success of Airbnb has been attributed to its creative solution for the accommodations market, but it has also been due to the founders' tenacity and willingness to keep going even in the face of adversity.

The three founders have been incredibly hands-on in the growth of the company, and have constantly sought out ways to innovate and make Airbnb better. They have also stayed focused on their original mission—to provide people with an affordable and accessible way to travel—and have never strayed too far from this goal.

Today, Airbnb stands as a testament to what can happen when you have a great idea, persevere through difficult times, and stay committed to your mission. It's a true success story that will continue to inspire aspiring entrepreneurs for many years to come.

Airbnb not only changed the way we think about travel accommodation, but it's opened up so many possibilities for both hosts and travelers alike. Hosts are able to earn extra income by renting out unused space or homes, while travelers are no longer limited by expensive hotel prices.

What's more, Airbnb offers an incomparable sense of community and hospitality; travelers often comment on how much they appreciate being welcomed into someone else's home or neighborhood.

It's inspiring to note that all this began with just three guys who saw a problem and created a unique solution. By turning that vision into reality, they've launched one of the most successful businesses in modern history.

Go reread the headline to this chapter. You need to fully embrace the idea that starting small can lead to great things – if you put enough effort into something and believe in it, there's no telling how far you can go!

And you are about to.

P.S. Airbnb listings include everything from private rooms and apartments, to entire homes, castles, boats, and treehouses. Meaning no matter what you are dealing with, success is possible as the result of learning and hard work.

Is Airbnb Hosting Right For You

Are you considering becoming an Airbnb host, but unsure if it is the right fit for you?

Of course, there are a few important factors to consider before taking the plunge as a host.

In this chapter, we will explore the pros and cons of Airbnb hosting so you can make an informed decision about whether or not it is the right fit for you. We will look at the financial requirements, potential earnings, and the necessary duties associated with becoming an Airbnb host. Having read this, you will have a clear understanding of whether Airbnb hosting is the right choice for you.

What is Airbnb?

Airbnb is a crazy=profitable online platform that allows people to rent out their properties to travelers to make as much or as little passive income as they seek to earn.

And your potential on it is limitless.

Remember that this company was started on a shoestring budget, a few air mattresses and a powerful two word headline on a crude, simple site.

Renters can easily search for available properties, view photos and descriptions, and make reservations without ever having to leave their homes. With Airbnb, hosts have access to a global network of guests from all over the world and have a huge opportunity to earn money and potentially big money from their properties.

All that said, it's super important to understand some of the risks and challenges associated with this type of rental business before toe hits water…so let's get to them now.

What are the benefits of being an Airbnb host?

Being an Airbnb host can be a great way to make extra income and have the flexibility of choosing when you want to host and who you want to host.

Without doubt, one of the biggest benefits of being an Airbnb host is the potential to make a considerable amount of money. Need convincing? According to Airbnb, hosts make up to $924 per month on average. That's on average.

Pushing deeper, aside from the financial rewards, hosting on Airbnb also allows you to interact with people from different cultures and backgrounds. Being an Airbnb host gives you the opportunity to get to know your guests, learn about their stories and explore new places which is a tremendous way for you to expand how you look at the world and the people in it.

Getting to the hosting particulars, Airbnb offers various levels of protection for hosts and provides insurance coverage in case something goes wrong. If a guest damages something while they're staying at your home, Airbnb will reimburse you up to a certain limit.

In all, hosting on Airbnb is an excellent way to build a strong personal brand as a host. Airbnb profiles offer detailed information about hosts so that potential guests can easily find someone who can meet their needs. Grasping that, you can quickly understand the importance of each and every interaction you have with your guests.

We'll get to that. Trust me.

Hosts have the ability to promote their listings through social media and other marketing platforms. In this history of time, there has never been a more exciting or demonstrable way to show off your properties than YouTube, Snap, Pinterest, Twitter, Facebook and all of the blog posts you will be putting out there.

This is your time like never before. Let that hit you hard.

As a stellar Airbnb host, you have full control over who stays at your home, how long they stay, and how much you charge them. You alone are able to set rules and expectations which help ensure a positive experience for both yourself and your guests. It also enables you to tailor your rental space to fit the type of visitors you are targeting.

As icing on that cake, Airbnb hosting requires very little setup compared to traditional rental properties. You don't need to worry about paperwork, inspections, maintenance, repairs, or dealing with tenants directly.

I told you this was killer, didn't I?

All these tasks are handled by Airbnb itself making it easier for you to focus on providing high quality hospitality experiences for your guests which in the end is the only thing that matters if you are going to scale this puppy up. And trust me, you are about to be scaling.

As long as you follow all relevant laws and regulations, communicate effectively with your guests, and keep up with maintenance requirements, it can be a great way to supplement your income and bring in extra revenue. Exceed expectations, be honest with your communicating and delivery and over deliver daily and you are a testimonial waiting to happen.

What are the drawbacks of being an Airbnb host?

Sure, that was all peachy. Love it, but lets get to the other side of that coin.

No problem.

Naturally, Airbnb hosting is not without its drawbacks. Firstly, it can be time-consuming and stressful to manage a rental property, even if you are just renting it out for short-term stays.

You will need to regularly check on the property and ensure it is clean and well maintained. This may require additional hours of work, especially if you don't live near the property.

You will also need to be available at all times to answer any questions from guests or to handle any complaints or issues. Please remember that there is no guarantee at all that your rental will be booked every night.

This means that you may have periods of time when the property is unoccupied, resulting in a loss of potential revenue. And you are not going to stand for that.

Without question, Airbnb hosts are required to pay local taxes and fees, including the short-term occupancy tax, which varies by city. You may also need to purchase liability insurance or other coverage to protect yourself in case of accidents or other incidents during a guest's stay.

Protection is paramount. 365.

Oh yeah, and even with great experiences, there is always the risk of negative reviews from guests, which can affect your reputation as a host and make it harder to book your property in the future.

Worry not. I will show you how to deal with those in the best way possible.

Let it also be clear that some homeowners' associations and rental complexes may prohibit short-term rentals altogether, so be sure to familiarize yourself with applicable laws and regulations before taking on an Airbnb hosting gig.

Eyes wide open is how you live now.

How much money can I make as an Airbnb host?

Aha...the good stuff. Finally! Expect to keep about 60% of every dollar you bring in.

But let me backtrack.

The amount of money you can make as an Airbnb host depends on a variety of factors, such as the location of your property, the number of guests you can accommodate, and the amenities you offer.

Just know that by going above and beyond with everything you do and how you present your properties you can always out distance yourself from anyone else in your area for the exact same location.

Remember the "I can outwork anyone" thing? Here it is and the long term branding you accomplish by white gloving your guests will mean endless and unstoppable bookings for years to come.

Point being push yourself to go white glove.

In the most general sense, the more desirable your property is, the more you can charge for it. The more services and amenities you offer, the more you can charge. Also, the more bookings you have, the more money you'll be able to make. See the pattern?

Finally, remember that in addition to the rental income you earn, Airbnb also charges a service fee of 3%, so make sure to factor that into your calculations when estimating how much money you can make from hosting on Airbnb.

You may also want to consider other expenses associated with hosting on Airbnb. These can include costs related to cleaning, laundry, maintenance, taxes, and insurance.

Please don't be naive as you head into this. Do your research and determine what additional costs might be involved in order to get an accurate picture of how much money you can make with Airbnb hosting.

Also important at this point is a careful consideration of how much time you will need to devote to being an Airbnb host. Hosting can require quite a bit of time, effort, and dedication depending on the size of your space, the amount of guest interaction required, and other responsibilities.

Finally, consider the potential risks associated with being an Airbnb host. Although unlikely, there is always the potential for bad reviews or dissatisfied customers. Take steps to minimize potential risks by following all laws and regulations, including those related to zoning restrictions, occupancy limits, safety protocols, etc.

Listen, I'd rather you have you come away from this book being pragmatic than having you be unrealistic about what you have to deal with.

How do I get started with Airbnb hosting?

Today, not tomorrow and not a week after your sister has her twins, today I want you to create a profile on Airbnb's website.

Deep breath. This is where you'll enter basic information about yourself, including your address and contact information. You'll also be asked to enter details about the type of accommodation you're offering, as well as other important information such as pricing and house rules.

You will suddenly feel as if you are in the Airbnb world and that is exactly the point...so no delays...do this for me right away.

Once you're in, you need to make sure your listing is complete and killer. This means adding great photos and powerful descriptions of your property, setting up your availability calendar, and establishing your booking policies.

If you have any additional amenities, such as Wi-Fi or a pool, you are not leaving those nuances out. Sell the sizzle. Sell the sizzle.

Once your listing is complete and hot, you start promoting it! Airbnb has a number of great tools that will help you reach potential guests, such as their "Experiences" feature, which allows you to list activities available in your area.

But it is on social media where you need to focus once you have maxed out your description and photos on the Airbnb site itself.

Get used to the idea that a great reputation is key, so providing outstanding customer service and ensuring that guests fully enjoy their stay will go a long way towards ensuring success.

And you are now no longer able to forget the fact that Airbnb encourages hosts to offer discounts or promotions to attract more guests. Wink, wink.

Without hesitation, it's crucial to remain aware of legal requirements specific to your area. Different countries and cities may require licenses or permits for short term rentals, so it's important to research these before beginning your venture into Airbnb hosting.

This is all on you and the more proactive you are hare, the far better,

Finally, please please please ensure that you have adequate insurance coverage that protects both you and your guests if something goes wrong. Researching different insurance options and choosing one that meets your needs is a huge step when considering Airbnb hosting.

You're Going To Crush It On Airbnb Here's How I Know

Story # 2

https://hopscotchtheglobe.com/airbnb-host-success-story/

Kristen and Siya from Ontario, Canada are free spirits who woke up one morning very concerned that they were suddenly no longer able to meet their bills and continue travelling the way they had.

They own a Swiss style, mountain top home close to the Canadian slopes and just a 2 minute drive to the village where there's on-going events happening year round.

As they themselves reveal, "we started to brainstorm other ways we could make money that would support our lifestyle and create a more passive income for us."

Kristen and Siya spent one day cleaning their house, taking photos and signing up to be a host.

And not too long after our listing went up, they received 13 enquiries in one day. And ended up making a sensational $10,000 in their first month.

As they learned more and more about Airbnb, they both came to find out that "even if you're renting your place, if you're able to sub-lease or have an agreement with your landlord, you can become an Airbnb host. That can be a tiny house, renovated RV, container house or Mongolian yurt."

And now that they are profitable Airbnb hosts, they are constantly thinking up ways to expand their business.

Their plan is also to build an additional guest house on their land in Costa Rica.

Choosing An Airbnb Business Structure

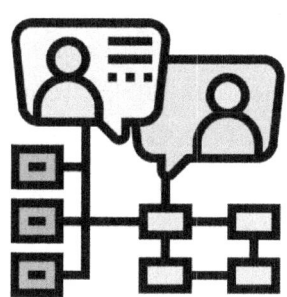

Getting hyped for what's ahead hosting? Good.

Allow me to provide you with a comprehensive overview of the various Airbnb business structures and the advantages and disadvantages of each. These are important.

In this jam packed chapter, we'll cover everything from sole proprietorships to LLCs and more, so that you can make the best decisions about which business structure is right for you and your Airbnb business.

What is an Airbnb Business?

An Airbnb business is a type of short-term rental that allows people to rent out their property for short stays. An Airbnb business can be used for both leisure and business travel, offering guests the chance to experience a different kind of accommodation than what is usually offered in hotels or hostels. (Which is exactly how it was started.)

The core concept behind an Airbnb business is quite simple: property owners rent out their home or apartment on a short-term basis to guests who are looking for a place to stay during their travels.

The rental period typically lasts from a few days to a few weeks, and can often be extended if needed. Property owners can set their own rates, terms and conditions, and house rules. They can also decide what kind of amenities they want to offer their guests, such as WiFi, kitchen facilities, etc. Hosts are in complete control, I need you to fully grasp that.

Most Airbnb businesses are run by individuals, but there are some larger companies that manage multiple properties at once. These companies offer more comprehensive services and can make the entire process easier and more profitable for property owners.

For your first rentals you are as of now prohibited from using any of those. I want you to know this process bit by nitty bit.

No matter how you choose to run your Airbnb business, it is important to remember that it is a hospitality business and that your guests' experience should always be your top priority.

As such, tell me it goes without saying that setting up clear house rules, providing a clean space, being responsive to inquiries and requests, and generally providing excellent customer service are more than essential components of running a successful Airbnb business.

What are the Different Types of Airbnb Businesses?

When it comes to running an Airbnb business, there are a variety of different structures to consider. The type of structure you choose for your business depends on many factors, including your personal preferences, the size of your business, and the regulations in your area.

So here is a breakdown of the different types of Airbnb businesses you can choose from.

Single Host: A single host is a person who rents out their own property and manages the day-to-day operations of the business.

Should be no stretch to realize that this type of business structure is suitable for people who are just starting out in the Airbnb business and want to manage their rental property on their own.

Property Management Company: Property management companies offer services such as cleaning, maintenance, customer service, and marketing to landlords who don't have the time or resources to manage their rental properties themselves.

This type of Airbnb business is ideal for larger Airbnb businesses that need help managing their rental properties on a daily basis. makes sense, right?

Real Estate Investment Company: Real estate investment companies purchase multiple rental properties and rent them out through the Airbnb platform. This type of Airbnb business is suitable for experienced investors who want to make money from multiple rental properties at once.

Rental Co-op: A rental co-op is a group of individuals or companies that come together to rent out their properties on the Airbnb platform. This type of Airbnb business allows members to share the workload and responsibility of managing their rental properties and gives them more flexibility in terms of setting their rental rates.

Franchise: Franchises offer franchisees access to a brand name, established operations and customer base, and a variety of services, such as marketing and customer service.

Yes, this type of Airbnb business is suitable for entrepreneurs who want to run a successful Airbnb business without having to start from scratch.

How to Choose the Right Airbnb Business Structure

Drilling into it, when it comes to starting an Airbnb business, the first thing you need to decide is what kind of structure you want your business to take.

There are a few different options available to you, each with its own set of advantages and disadvantages. Understanding the different business structures and how they work is essential if you want to choose the right one for your particular needs.

The most common types of Airbnb businesses include sole proprietorships, partnerships, limited liability companies (LLCs), and corporations. Each has its own set of tax and legal implications, as well as its own benefits and drawbacks. Here's a quick overview of each option:

Sole Proprietorship: A sole proprietorship is the simplest form of business structure and does not require any formal paperwork or registration. As the owner of a sole proprietorship, you'll be personally liable for all debts, obligations, and liabilities that your business incurs.

This means that any potential losses incurred by your business will come out of your personal finances. Easy to understand, huh?

Partnership: A partnership is similar to a sole proprietorship in that there are no formal paperwork or registration requirements. The difference lies in the fact that there is more than one person involved in the ownership of the business. Partners in a partnership are personally responsible for all debts, obligations, and liabilities of the business.

Limited Liability Company (LLC): An LLC is a hybrid legal entity that provides its owners with limited personal liability. This means that you will not be held personally liable for any debts or other obligations that your business incurs. It also allows you to have more flexibility when it comes to taxation.

Corporation: A corporation is a more complex form of business structure than either a sole proprietorship or a partnership. It requires formal paperwork and registration and also limits the liability of its owners.

This means that even if your business incurs debts or obligations, your personal assets will not be at risk. However, corporations are also subject to double taxation—both corporate income tax and individual income tax.

Each type of Airbnb business structure has its own unique set of advantages and disadvantages. Consider your specific needs and situation carefully before making a decision as to which structure is right for you. Think about things like taxation, personal liability, ease of setup, and other factors before making your choice.

The Pros and Cons of Each Airbnb Business Structure

Since you are now starting an Airbnb business, one of the most important decisions you'll need to make is choosing the right business structure. Each type of Airbnb business comes with its own pros and cons, and it's important to weigh them carefully before making a decision.

LLC: An LLC, or limited liability company, is a popular choice for Airbnb businesses because it provides a great level of protection for the business owner. It limits their personal liability and can provide tax advantages over other business structures. One of the drawbacks is that it's more expensive and complicated to set up than other business structures.

Sole Proprietorship: A sole proprietorship is a business owned and run by one individual. This is the simplest and least expensive form of business structure, but it also provides the owner with no personal liability protection.

Partnership: A partnership is a business owned and run by two or more people. This structure is more complex than a sole proprietorship and requires more paperwork, but it also offers more protection to each partner than a sole proprietorship does.

Corporation: A corporation is a business owned by shareholders who elect a board of directors to make decisions on their behalf. This structure offers the most liability protection, but it's also the most expensive and complicated to set up.

No matter which type of Airbnb business structure you choose, it's important to understand the pros and cons before making a decision. Understanding your options will help you make an informed decision about the best way to structure your Airbnb business.

Which Airbnb Business Structure is Right for You?

Naturally, when it comes to choosing the right Airbnb business structure for you, there is no one-size-fits-all answer. Each unique option has its own set of pros and cons that need to be weighed very carefully.

In my humble opinion, the best approach is to evaluate your current situation, your long-term goals, and the resources available to you in order to make an informed decision. And again, be honest with yourself and your goals.

If you are new to Airbnb hosting, the most popular option is often the sole proprietorship. This structure is the simplest and easiest to set up, as there is no need to register a business or create separate legal entities. Furthermore, all profits are reported on your personal tax returns, making the filing process straightforward and stress-free. However, this structure also leaves you vulnerable to personal liability, meaning that any debts or claims against your business could put your personal assets at risk.

For those who are looking for more protection from personal liability, incorporating your Airbnb business may be the best option. Forming an LLC or Corporation gives you greater flexibility with taxes, as well as greater protection from personal liability. Incorporating also allows you to separate your business finances from your personal finances, creating a clearer financial picture for tax purposes.

However, incorporating also requires additional paperwork and compliance measures that need to be followed, which can be time-consuming and complex.

Finally, you may want to consider forming a partnership if you plan to share the responsibilities of running your Airbnb business with someone else. A partnership allows two or more people to form a single business entity, with each partner responsible for their own portion of the business's profits and losses.

Know that this structure requires additional paperwork and can be difficult to manage without a formal agreement outlining each partner's responsibilities.

How to Conduct Airbnb Market Research Like A Seasoned Pro

Let's go ahead and talk turkey about how to maximize the potential of your Airbnb business from day 1 starting with your market research.

In this very chapter, I will go ahead and provide you with some tips and tricks on how to conduct market research like a pro, and give you the inside scoop on the best Airbnb secrets for doing so.

Cue the music!

Know your target market

It is critical to understand who your target market is when conducting Airbnb market research. Not guessing but knowing who your target market is will easily help you determine which strategies will be the most effective in reaching those potential customers.

When you are out there researching your target market, consider such factors as age, gender, geographic location, interests and income level. Sounds so simple but by understanding your target market, you can tailor your marketing strategies to reach them more effectively each and every time you host.

Know if your guests prefer a certain style of accommodation? Are they looking for a home away from home experience or do they want an economical option? Without question, knowing the answers to these exact questions will 100% help you design a strategy that will reach your target market in the most effective way.

And that is what we strive for each and every day, right?

It bears noting that it is important to always remember that your target market can change over time. Be sure to monitor trends and conduct regular surveys of your target market to ensure that you are still targeting the right people. Flexibility, kids, Flexibility.

Open your windows and look at your competitors

Look at precisely what they are doing before you jump into any market. In the case of Airbnb, that means taking a look at what other rental properties in your area are offering and pricing their services at.

One way to do this is to look at each competitor's website, social media accounts, and any other information they've made public. If the web is one thing, it is transparent...and that plays right into your hands. Work it.

Compare their amenities and prices, and see if there are any unique features that stand out. Are they offering discounts or promotions? Are they advertising on local radio or TV? You can also look at review sites like TripAdvisor or Yelp to get an idea of how they're performing with customers.

Dig.

You can also look at the online marketplace as a whole to get an idea of the trends in the industry. Sites like Airbnb often release their own data on market trends that can be useful for understanding the big picture.

Being diligent and organized as hell here will help you determine which cities or neighborhoods have the most demand for rental properties, as well as which types of rental properties are more popular. Facts will pop. You will know in short order what's what in your neck of the woods so to speak.

Find your niche

Starting this afternoon, you need to find a niche that sets you apart from the competition. This can be anything from providing pet-friendly lodging, to offering luxury amenities, to catering to a specific target audience. Simple to do, but a must: research your competitors and see what they are not offering.

Easy peasy. Once you know what other Airbnb owners are missing, you can tailor your services to provide what these customers are looking for. You may decide to offer more luxurious linens, provide pet-friendly lodging, or specialize in marketing to business travelers. The goal is simple, make sure you offer something that sets you apart from the competition.

You should also consider how you will be able to attract more potential customers through advertising. Consider running targeted campaigns on Facebook or using Google AdWords to reach customers who might be interested in your services. As a side note, if you do go this route, use someone or a service that you trust, The amount of click fraud online is wicked.

Every night before head meets pillow, make sure that you are regularly updating and refreshing your listings on the Airbnb website. Keeping your listings up to date with the latest information, photos, and amenities will ensure that guests have all the information they need when considering a stay at your Airbnb property.

Oh no, no no. We are not here to be any kind of reasonable alternative, we are here to be better than anyone else in everything we do as hosts. Nothing less.

Use social media

Forget memes and crap photos of a Kardashian picnic, social media is an unreal tool for you to get your market research. Social sites can provide you with real-time data about the trends and interests of your target audience. With the right strategy, you can use social media to create meaningful connections with your potential customers and gain valuable insight into their behavior. We want this.

To start, create profiles on popular social media platforms like Facebook, Twitter, Instagram, and LinkedIn. And don't pass up Pinterest where photos rule! You can then use these profiles to reach out to potential customers, build relationships, and get a better understanding of their interests and needs.

Once you have established a presence on these platforms, begin to analyze data related to your target market. This can include things such as the type of content they're engaging with, how often they're posting, and what types of topics they're discussing. This will help you better understand your target audience and their preferences.

Again the transparency on social platforms is there for the taking. Take it.

You can also use social media to keep track of what competitors are doing in your market. This includes following their pages, joining relevant industry conversations, and staying up-to-date with the latest trends in your sector. Doing so will help you spot opportunities to differentiate your business from the competition.

Want to seriously step it up? Consider leveraging influencers to promote your Airbnb listing or service. Connecting with influencers in your niche can help you reach new audiences and increase visibility for your business. This is what heavy hitting marketers in every niche do daily.

You're Going To Crush It On Airbnb Here's How I Know

TREEHOUSE AIRBNB STORY

STORY # 3

How to Create House Rules for Your Airbnb Listing

As a pie-eyed new Airbnb host, you 're probably wondering how to create house rules for your listing. Guess what...setting up clear and reasonable house rules is an important part of hosting on Airbnb, as it ensures your guests know what is expected of them and can help prevent any potential issues or disputes.

From the basics of what to include in your rules, to setting out expectations for behavior, cleaning, and more, I say we cover everything you need to know to ensure your house rules are successful.

All those in favor?

Keep it Short and Simple

Short and sweet wins. Period.

When creating house rules for your Airbnb listing, remember to keep them short and simple. This way, guests will be more likely to read and understand the rules that you are setting. Be sure to include only the most important rules, and leave out any information that isn't absolutely necessary.

Make sure that your language is easy to understand, and avoid using jargon or complicated terms. Your Airbnb house rules should be as straightforward as possible so that your guests will be able to quickly understand and follow them.

Use positive language in your rules whenever possible; this helps ensure that your rules remain professional and inviting. Additionally, provide clear explanations for each rule to explain why it is in place. You may also want to mention what potential consequences could occur if a guest fails to abide by the rules. Better upfront than after the police show up in the middle of the night.

Write in a Friendly Tone

When creating your Airbnb house rules, use a super friendly and welcoming tone. After all, these rules should be there to make guests feel safe and comfortable, not scared or threatened.

Oh that's right, your Airbnb guests are people too and that you want them to enjoy their stay.

When writing your house rules, use words like "please" and "thank you" to indicate that you're friendly and appreciative of their presence. Also, be sure to keep the language casual and informal as this will help make them feel more at ease.

Instead of saying something like "You must not..." say something like "We kindly ask that..."

The difference between those two is night and day, trust me.

At the end of the day, your house rules should be there to protect both you and your guests. Write them in a way that is both clear and friendly, and you'll be sure to create an enjoyable stay for everyone involved. It's also important to include information about amenities and services you provide so that guests know exactly what they can expect from their stay.

Make sure to include details such as whether pets are allowed on the premises, if smoking is allowed, what time check-in and check-out is, etc.

Also, remember to include information about any restrictions on noise levels or any other activities that could cause a disturbance for your neighbors or other guests.

Additionally, consider adding information about parking if necessary - some areas may have regulations on when and where cars can park, so make sure you include these restrictions in your house rules.

Don't forget to emphasize any safety measures you've taken, such as smoke detectors, fire extinguishers, etc., so guests know they're in good hands while they're staying with you. Finally, let guests know how they can contact you if they have any questions or concerns during their stay. The importance of this can never be overstated. Your guests need to have access...give it to them.

Cover the Essentials

When writing your Airbnb house rules, it's important to include the essential points that your guests need to know.

This can include things like:

No smoking indoors

No pets allowed

Quiet hours from 10 pm-8 am

No parties or events

Parking rules and restrictions

Check-in and check-out times

Whether or not guests are allowed to use the kitchen

Whether or not guests are allowed to access the yard or balcony

Be sure to specify what items you do and don't allow in your listing (like candles, incense, etc.)

These are just some of the key points that you should include in your house rules.

Outline any potential hazards on the property and how best to avoid them.

You may also want to include a few additional considerations that may not fit into the standard categories. For example, if you live in a multi-unit building, you may want to include a reminder about respecting common spaces such as shared hallways, stairwells, and elevators. You may also want to add instructions about disposing of trash properly. Details matter.

Finally, think about including a list of amenities that may be available at your rental property such as Wi-Fi networks or cable channels. A comprehensive set of house rules will help ensure that both yourself and your guests stay safe and comfortable during their stay.

Always ask yourself "how would I like to be treated at an Airbnb?"

Give Guests an Incentive to Follow the Rules

Offering an incentive to guests for following your house rules can be a great way to ensure they're taken seriously and followed. Depending on the type of incentive, you can use it as a tool to encourage guests to follow the rules and stay safe during their stay.

Like examples? Okay, here's a good one. You may offer a complimentary amenity or service to guests who follow your house rules. Some ideas for amenities include: a bottle of wine or champagne, a welcome snack basket, a small gift card, free breakfast, or a voucher for a local attraction or restaurant.

These go miles and miles.

You can also provide incentives for leaving the property in a clean and tidy condition when they check out. These could include discounts on future stays or a special thank you gift.

Incentives like these can help remind guests of your house rules and give them a positive reason to follow them. It also shows that you value your guests and are committed to providing them with a pleasant and memorable experience. Setting up house rules helps to protect both the guest and host from liability issues, should something go wrong during the stay.

To go above and beyond (which is how you will be operating) in addition to listing your house rules in your Airbnb profile, make sure to discuss any specific requests or guidelines at the beginning of each guest's stay.

Make sure they know where things are located and how certain items should be used properly. If there are any areas of the home that are off-limits, such as certain rooms or outdoor spaces, explain this clearly to your guests so there are no misunderstandings.

Finally, set up reminders throughout the home to keep guests informed about any safety guidelines, such as not entering certain areas without permission, or not tampering with equipment.

Imagine that. Clarity rules the roost. Who knew?

Include Contact Information

When you create house rules for your Airbnb listing, it's monstrously important to provide contact information so that guests can reach you if they have questions or concerns. Make sure that you include both your email address and phone number in the house rules section.

You should also make it clear how you prefer to be contacted. Some hosts may want guests to call them first before sending an email, while others may prefer the opposite. Whatever you decide, make sure that this is stated clearly in the house rules section.

In addition, you should also let guests know who else they can contact if you are unavailable. If you use a property manager or other third-party service, provide their contact information in the house rules as well. Prepare for everything contingency with contact availability.

Making sure that your contact information is readily available to guests will help to resolve any issues or questions quickly and effectively. Include Check-In and Check-Out Times:

At the very top of the list of things to include you simply must make sure that you specify check-in and check-out times in your Airbnb house rules. It's up to your rules to ensure that everyone is on the same page about when guests are expected to arrive and leave.

If you need to change these times after publishing your listing, be sure to update the house rules accordingly. Also, specify whether you offer early check-in and late check-out, and include any additional fees associated with these services.

You're Going To Crush It On Airbnb Here's How I Know

Story 3

https://financebuzz.com/secrets-of-successful-airbnb-host

Vincent Brue, 40, and his wife, Eve, 38, purchased their four-bedroom Long Branch, New Jersey home in 2010, knowing that it offered a bit more space than they needed.

The two video editors fell in love with the Jersey location, which is an easy 10-minute walk to the beach and less than a mile from a thriving oceanfront shopping and dining center.

But after years of renting to revolving roommates, the pair opted to give Airbnb a try.

Switching to Airbnb skyrocketed their income from $15,000 per year to $30,000.

"We started Airbnb-ing the three extra bedrooms in our house in October 2016, after almost six years of longer-term rentals, and found it to be much better financially and personally," said Vincent. "So far, we've netted almost $90,000,

and that was with us occupying the entire second floor of the home."

"I think the most important thing is to be extremely clear to guests about every little detail of the experience, from directions to the home, to check-in/check-out, and house rules," Vincent says.

The Brue's, who are now Superhosts, have since welcomed more than 500 Airbnb guests.

Though the Brues have been thrilled with their decision to become Airbnb hosts,

Vincent noted that it can require quite a bit of time and energy depending on the season.

The couple now dedicates between 20 to 30 hours per week to their side hustle during the busy season,

and about five to 10 hours in the off-season. Up to this point, the Brues have handled all the work themselves.

With the newly found income, the couple recently bought and moved into a smaller house just a few miles away.

How to Create the Perfect Airbnb House Manual

Now that you are an Airbnb host, know that creating a house manual is an essential part of welcoming your guests. Not only does a house manual provide your guests with vital information about your property and its amenities, but it also serves as a reminder of the house rules, check-in procedures, and any other important details.

The basics of an Airbnb house manual

Having a house manual is essential for successful hosting on Airbnb. It is essentially a guide to the home that can be easily accessed by guests who are staying in your property.

Your manual should include information about the check-in and check-out process, amenities, local attractions and activities, house rules, emergency contact information, and anything else that might help a guest feel comfortable and welcome during their stay.

Here are some of the basics of creating an effective Airbnb house manual:

1. Set up an online document or PDF: An online document or PDF is an easy way to make sure that your manual is easily accessible to your guests. You can link to the document from your listing, or simply email it to guests after they book.
2. Make sure all the basics are included: Include details such as check-in and check-out times, emergency contact numbers, Wi-Fi passwords, house rules, parking information, and any local attractions or activities that may be of interest to your guests.
3. Think about practical matters: List where the trash bins are located, how to use appliances and electronics, and any other details that may be helpful during a guest's stay.
4. Consider adding more personal touches: A few welcoming words, an introduction to the area, some local tips and advice, and even a few photos can make your house manual even more inviting and useful for guests.

What to include in your manual

1. Introduction: Introduce yourself and your home to your guests, provide a warm welcome and any information they need about you, the house, and the neighborhood.
2. Check-in: Include all of the necessary information for check-in, such as check-in time, how to access the keys, and any other details regarding their arrival.
3. House rules: Establish the house rules and expectations for your guests in a clear manner. Be sure to outline the basics like quiet hours, no smoking, and no pets.

4. Wi-Fi: Provide your guests with the Wi-Fi password, along with any other information they may need to get online.

5. House amenities: List all of the amenities you offer in your home, such as kitchen appliances, hot tubs or pools, and other features.

6. Emergency contact information: Provide your guests with emergency contact information in case they need to reach out while they're staying at your home.

7. Local attractions: Give your guests a list of local attractions and places to visit, so they can make the most out of their stay.

8. Housekeeping: Give clear instructions for housekeeping during their stay, such as when garbage and recycling should be taken out and how to report any problems or issues during their stay.

9. Check-out: Outline the check-out process and provide any necessary information such as checkout times and key drop-off details,

I should not have to say this since you have heard this already but keep your manual up-to-date - if something changes at your property (like a new appliance being added), it has to be reflected in your house manual.

Keep an updated version of your manual that reflects these changes.

You may also want to consider using an app or website to store your house manual; this way, it's easier for both you and your guests to access it.

How to format your manual

When you're creating a house manual for your Airbnb guests, it's important to consider the format of the document.

1. Use plain language – Keep your language simple and straightforward. Avoid industry jargon, and instead explain concepts in an easy-to-understand way.
2. Break it up into sections – A house manual can quickly become overwhelming. Help your guests by breaking the document up into sections and subsections. This will make it easier to find specific information.
3. Use visuals – Incorporate visuals whenever possible to make the document more engaging. Include pictures or diagrams of specific amenities or instructions, or even maps of the area.
4. Use bullet points – To make it easier to scan and digest the information, use bullet points whenever possible.
5. Add white space – Don't cram too much text onto one page. Add plenty of white space between sections, paragraphs, and bullet points to help your guests take it all in.

By following these tips, you can create a house manual that is informative, easy to read, and well-organized. Your guests will constantly appreciate having all of the information they need in one place, allowing them to have a comfortable and stress-free stay.

Think about it, this is what the best hotels offer.

Remember to include recommendations for local attractions, restaurants, grocery stores, etc. Be sure to clearly spell out any rules and expectations you may have as a host so there are no surprises or misunderstandings during their visit.

Go ahead and invite feedback from past guests on ways to improve the manual. This feedback can provide valuable insights into what works and what doesn't. And do not be afraid to let your guests know where they can access the house manual during their visit; consider including a link on your listing's website or emailing it directly to each guest before their arrival.

Go beyond. Role reverse and just watch what happens with your own expectations.

Airbnb Business Expenses: A Guide to What You Can Deduct

Okay, here is an absolute must for Airbnb hosts looking to maximize profits by understanding the tax deductions that are available.

Here's a comprehensive guide to understanding and utilizing your Airbnb business expenses, so that you can get the most out of your hosting business.

I will explain exactly which expenses are deductible, how to keep track of them, and how to use them to reduce your taxes. By the end of this chapter, you will be well-equipped to take advantage of the deductions available to you as an Airbnb host.

Cha-ching.

Advertising

Advertising costs are critical when it comes to becoming a successful Airbnb host and business. As a business owner, you may be able to deduct the cost of any advertising you use to promote your rental space.

To be clear, we are now talking about any costs related to creating and displaying advertisements on websites, newspapers, or other mediums. You can also deduct any fees associated with listing your rental on a booking platform or website.

Any as long as they are relevant and you have proof of them.

When calculating your advertising expenses, that's the time to include the cost of the advertisement itself, as well as the cost of any materials used to create it (such as paper, ink, etc.).

And you probably know this but when you hire a professional to design and/or manage your advertisements, you can deduct the cost of their services as well.

Keep in mind that if you receive any discounts on your advertising expenses, such as reduced rates for bulk purchases, you must subtract those discounts from your total cost before deducting the amount from your taxes.

Finally, if you use online advertising platforms such as Google AdWords or Facebook Ads, you can deduct the amount that you paid for the ad itself, but not any additional expenses like clicks or impressions.

Almost forgot this, keep track of how much time you spent creating and managing your ads — this is considered labor and can be deducted too. Just make sure to document your time properly so that you have evidence if needed.

In addition to advertising costs, there are a few other types of deductions you should consider when calculating your Airbnb business expenses.

If you have office supplies dedicated exclusively to running your Airbnb business, those items would qualify for deduction. Other deductible items might include travel expenses incurred while scouting out potential listings, hosting supplies purchased exclusively for the purpose of providing guests with items they might need during their stay, and any necessary tools or equipment required to maintain your rental property.

Guess what, all of this adds up, folks.

PS. Don't forget about energy costs — these often go overlooked, but they can add up quickly!

Cleaning and Maintenance

When it comes to running a successful Airbnb, regular cleaning and maintenance is essential for keeping your property in top condition.

Happily, all the associated costs of cleaning and maintaining your rental property are tax deductible. This includes the cost of cleaning supplies, hiring a professional cleaner, and any repairs that may be needed.

To make sure you get the most out of your deductions, make sure to keep all your receipts for cleaning supplies, and invoices for any services you may have hired. Be sure and track the time you spend on cleaning and maintenance yourself. This way, you'll have a comprehensive record of your expenses come tax season.

Does it end there? Nope. Some other maintenance-related business expenses can be deducted as well. These include landscaping fees, pest control fees, heating and cooling bills, utility bills, alarm systems, security cameras, appliance repair bills, insurance premiums, and more. Play 100% fair with the good old IRS and remember that these expenses must all directly relate to your Airbnb business for them to qualify as deductions.

Depreciation

To be sure, depreciation is a big expense to consider when it comes to running a successful Airbnb business. This is a non-cash expense that is used to spread out the cost of large purchases such as furniture, appliances, and other long-term investments over their useful life. This helps reduce your taxable income and can be claimed as a deduction each year.

When it comes to calculating depreciation, you will need to consider the useful life of the item and the cost basis of the item. The cost basis is the original price of the item minus any discounts or trade-ins. You should also factor in any repairs or upgrades you make to the item.

If it's late and your tired, remember that this book was written to open your eyes to all of these new things for you to be considering...I want those eyes open!

To determine the useful life of an item, look up the IRS guidelines for depreciation of that type of asset.

There are two different methods of calculating depreciation, the straight-line method and the declining balance method. You can easily find out about those on your own in terms of your Airbnb properties.

Just know that depreciation is an important expense to consider when it comes to running an Airbnb business, and it is a must now that you know how to calculate it correctly.

I can't sing loud enough the importance of, having and keeping accurate financial records. Do it from the very beginning because no one wants to hear me sing. Ewwww.

No matter what type of business you run, being aware of expenses related to your Airbnb business is essential for success. Understanding which expenses are deductible and what types of credits may be available can help you stay on top of your finances and help ensure that your Airbnb business stays profitable and thriving.

Which yours is about to be.

Insurance

When running a business, insurance is a must and Airbnb hosts are no exception. Having the right insurance coverage protects both you and your property and allows you to continue running your business without interruption.

Some of the most common insurance policies that Airbnb hosts purchase are:

- • Homeowners or renters insurance: This will protect your home and personal belongings in case of damage or theft caused by guests. It's important to note that homeowners or renters insurance will not cover any income lost due to cancellations or disputes, and most policies do not cover business activities.

- • Host protection insurance: This is a type of liability insurance offered by Airbnb. It covers up to $1 million in damages caused by guests, including personal injury and property damage, but does not cover income lost due to cancellations or disputes.
- • Business liability insurance: If you have any employees working for you, such as cleaners or landscapers, it's important to have business liability insurance to protect yourself against potential lawsuits.
- • Professional indemnity insurance: This policy will cover you in the event of a professional negligence claim, such as if your guest gets sick from something you served them at your property or if they experience a burglary while staying with you.
- • Property damage insurance: This will protect you in case of damage to your property caused by a guest. This includes damage to furniture, appliances, walls, floors, and other physical property in the home.

It is more important than you will ever know that you have the right insurance coverage in place before a single guest is settled in.

You need to know that you are fully covered in case of an any unexpected accidents or issues at your Airbnb. Please go speak with an insurance expert who can provide advice tailored to your specific situation.

Depending on where you live, different laws may apply when it comes to what kind of insurance you need for your Airbnb business. Additionally, there may be local ordinances that require specific insurance coverage depending on where your rental is located.

Finally, consider signing up for rental management services which often come bundled with specialized insurance packages designed specifically for rental properties like Airbnbs.

These packages include coverages such as public liability, employer's liability, legal expenses, and product liability among others. Ultimately, having the right insurance in place will give you peace of mind when it comes to protecting yourself and your rental property should anything go wrong.

You getting all this? The right insurance is a must have. No skimping here.

Interest

When it comes to interest, Airbnb business owners need to keep track of all of their costs from day 1.

This includes any loans taken out to purchase the rental property, mortgages, credit cards, and other forms of financing used for the business.

Depending on the type of loan taken out, you may be able to deduct any interest that was incurred. If you took out a loan specifically for your Airbnb business, then you will most likely be able to deduct this interest. This is huge.

By the way, if you are using a credit card for your Airbnb business expenses, you will be able to deduct the applicable interest payments. As always, make absolutely sure to save all records of your interest payments so that you can accurately report them when filing your taxes.

Some other expenses that may be deductible include maintenance costs, insurance premiums, marketing fees, travel expenses related to inspecting or managing the rental property, legal fees, cleaning services, and furnishings. Maintenance costs such as repairs or replacements should also be kept track of in order to properly itemize these deductions.

To make matters even better, insurance premiums related to the property should also be tracked as they too can be deducted from your income tax. Marketing fees such as those associated with advertising or running promotions may also be eligible for deduction.

No missing those interest deductions! You got me?

Legal and Professional Fees

Legal and professional fees are a necessary part of running a successful Airbnb business. They include everything from setting up an LLC or corporation to obtaining necessary licenses, to drafting contracts with your guests and landlords.

When it comes to legal and professional fees, it is important to make sure that you are properly documenting all the expenses you incur. Any expense over $600 should be tracked and reported as a separate line item on your taxes. This includes attorney fees, accounting services, and any other professional service you may need to run your business.

My advice: get good at organizing asap.

If you are just getting started, you may want to consider working with an experienced lawyer to ensure you have all the necessary legal paperwork in place before launching your Airbnb business. They can help you understand any local zoning regulations and ensure that your business is in compliance with them.

As your business grows, you may need additional legal advice or assistance on various aspects of running your Airbnb business. Yes, you can deduct any fees paid for legal counsel or advice related to operating your Airbnb business, so make sure you keep track of these costs.

Again, organize.

Finally, you may also want to consider investing in legal protection coverage from a third-party provider. This type of insurance can help protect you from certain types of liability or lawsuits related to your Airbnb business.

Depending on your provider, you may be able to deduct the cost of this coverage as well. It's always best to consult a tax expert or accountant to determine what deductions are available to you when filing your tax return.

You should also consider making quarterly estimated tax payments throughout the year if you expect to owe more than $1,000 in taxes when you file. Huge insight here: quarterly payments allow you to spread out the amount owed over four installments throughout the year instead of having to pay the entire amount at once when filing.

Go quarterly. You can thank me later.

Taxes

As with everything on earth, taxes are a major part of running an Airbnb business. As a host, you are responsible for ensuring that all taxes associated with your rental are paid in full.

When it comes to taxes, there are two main categories that you need to consider: state and federal taxes. Depending on the laws in your area, you may also need to pay local taxes as well.

For state and federal taxes, you will typically be required to pay income taxes on the income that you generate from renting out your space. You can deduct certain expenses associated with running your Airbnb, such as cleaning and maintenance costs, from this income before calculating how much tax you owe.

When it comes to local taxes, these vary by location. In some places, hosts may be required to pay taxes on their Airbnb income or additional taxes for each stay. Make sure to research the specific laws in your area to ensure that you are compliant with all local tax regulations.

Organization and precision are a must here. So to keep track of all of your Airbnb business expenses and help make sure that you don't miss any important tax deadlines, it is a terribly good idea to use a reliable accounting software like QuickBooks.

That simple to use software will help you stay organized and save time when it comes time to file your taxes. My favorite thing here is that using accounting software can help you easily identify deductions that you can take advantage of so that you end up paying the minimum amount of tax possible.

For example, let's say you rent out multiple properties through Airbnb. Let's further say that you may be able to deduct the cost of items purchased to improve those properties, such as furniture or appliances. Also, if you hire someone to help manage your listings, you may be able to deduct their wages and other associated costs.

On top of state, federal, and local taxes, there are a few other expenses related to running an Airbnb business that you should factor into your budget. These include things like insurance premiums, advertising fees, credit card processing fees, and other miscellaneous costs.

Finally, if you rent out a single property but still incur significant travel-related expenses (such as gas money), you may be able to deduct those expenses under "ordinary and necessary" deductions provided by the IRS.

I hope you are getting a sense of the scale of the things you will need to attend to as you roar to 6 and then possibly seven figures with Airbnb.

Utilities

When it comes to running a successful Airbnb business, it's important to be aware of the various expenses you can incur when it comes to utilities. Utilities can include electricity, water, heating, and cooling. Depending on the type of rental property you own, you may be responsible for some or all of these expenses.

Electricity: If you are renting out your home and you have an individual electricity meter installed in your property, then you will be able to claim any energy costs associated with your Airbnb business as a business expense. It's important to note that if you share a meter with other occupants, then you cannot claim their electricity costs as part of your business expenses.

Water

Most landlords are responsible for supplying their tenants with water for the duration of their stay. However, if you are responsible for paying for the water bill, then you can claim this cost as a business expense.

Heating and Cooling

If your rental property has an HVAC system (heating, ventilation, and air conditioning), then you can claim the cost of running this system as a business expense. This includes any repairs, maintenance, or replacement of the HVAC system.

It's important to keep accurate records of all utility bills associated with your Airbnb business in order to ensure you are claiming all relevant expenses and reducing your taxable income.

Additionally, you should also look into tax credits or deductions that may be available to help reduce your tax burden even further. For example, there may be local energy tax credits available for businesses that use renewable sources of energy such as solar panels.

Additionally, investing in energy-efficient appliances such as high-efficiency washers and dryers can help reduce your monthly operating costs.

Finally, you should always consult with a tax professional to make sure you're taking advantage of all available deductions and credits. With the right strategies in place, understanding your Airbnb business expenses can help minimize your tax liability while maximizing your profits.

How I Know You'll Crush It On Airbnb
Here's How I Know

Story #4

https://www.airbnb.com/d/rent-or-airbnb-success-story

The Top 10 Airbnb Hosting Mistakes to Avoid

If you're an Airbnb host, it's so much more than important to make sure you're doing everything possible to make your guests' experience as pleasant and stress-free as possible. However, even the most experienced Airbnb hosts can make mistakes that can hurt their bottom line.

Cue the horrifying music track.

To help you avoid some of the common Airbnb hosting mistakes, I've put together a list of the top 10 Airbnb hosting mistakes to avoid.

1) Not being clear about your cancellation policy

One of the most important things to consider when hosting on Airbnb is having a clear cancellation policy in place. This policy should be clearly outlined in your listing so that guests understand what happens if they need to cancel their reservation. The two most common policies are strict and moderate, each with their own set of rules and restrictions.

Strict policies offer little to no flexibility for guests and require them to pay all or part of the cost of their reservation if they decide to cancel within a certain amount of time. Moderate policies are more lenient and may allow for some flexibility for guests, depending on the situation.

Regardless of which policy you choose, it's important to make sure your guests understand your rules and are aware of any fees they might incur if they need to cancel.

You can also provide additional information such as travel insurance options and contact information in case they have any questions or concerns. This will help ensure that all parties involved have a better understanding of the terms and conditions, minimizing any potential issues.

Another mistake many hosts make is not taking proper precautions against scams.

Although Airbnb does its best to protect hosts from fraud, scammers still manage to get through the system. When it comes to protecting yourself from fraud, there are several steps you can take, including running background checks on potential guests and using trusted payment methods such as PayPal or Stripe.

I know this may sound harsh, but your safety and your business success is what is most important to me. Return the favor and do your homework on your guests...because I could easily point you to several hundred horrifying Airbnb hosting stories.

Remember to not accept cash payments from guests and never give out personal information.

Take the time to familiarize yourself with the laws and regulations in your area regarding short-term rentals. These laws vary by city, state, and country. Not doing this could lead to costly fines or even legal action against you.

2) Not providing enough information about the space

One of the other biggest mistakes you can make as an Airbnb host is not providing enough information about the space you are offering. You should make sure to clearly list the size of the accommodation, any amenities that come with it, and any rules or expectations you have for your guests.

It is up to no one but you to make sure to provide detailed descriptions of the space and its features, as well as any restrictions on use.

If you have a common area or shared facilities, make sure to also provide information on how those areas can be used. Be sure to also list any items that are included in the space, such as towels, linens, and kitchen supplies. Use that friendly accommodating tone, be specific and clear.

3) Not having good quality photos

When it comes to Airbnb hosting at the highest level, one of the biggest mistakes you can make is not having good quality photos. Happens far more than you know and it should never happen.

Nothing less than amazing photos that showcase your space in the best possible light and provide potential guests with a clear understanding of what your Airbnb looks like. Poor quality photos are garbage and beneath you.

Never use them.

Ensure that all of your photos are clear, high-resolution, and taken in natural lighting. If you're taking your own photos, you may want to invest in a decent camera and use a tripod or other stabilizing device so that they look professional.

Make sure that your photos accurately reflect the size and layout of the space. Try to capture photos from different angles, such as overhead shots and close-ups. And, don't forget to showcase any special features or amenities your space has to offer. Great photos are your greatest asset before the booking,

Promise me you will max them out.

4) Not communicating with guests before their arrival

When hosting on Airbnb, you simply have got to keep in communication with your guests before they arrive. Make sure you provide clear instructions on how to get to your space and the check-in procedure.

Not communicating with guests can lead to confusion and misunderstandings, so be sure to set expectations and answer any questions ahead of time.

5) Not being available during their stay

Not if but when you are hosting on Airbnb, it is important to be available to your guests during their stay. This means being available to answer any questions they may have or provide assistance in the event of an emergency.

6) Not having a backup plan for if something goes wrong

Let me be blunt right about here and let you know that it is important to have a backup plan if something goes wrong when hosting on Airbnb. This could include a plan for dealing with late check-ins, unruly guests, or unforeseen circumstances.

For example, if you're hosting an event, make sure you have a contingency plan in case your guests are late or cause any issues. If you have unexpected guests arrive, it's best to have an alternative accommodation in case you can't accommodate them. Plan for the unexpected…that is what super hosts have come to do without blinking.

Sounds rough, but you also need a plan for how to handle refunds in the event of something going wrong. If there's a power outage or some other incident that requires you to cancel the reservation, you should know what steps to take to refund the guest.

Finally, for the less than sellar reviews, it's important to have a plan for dealing with reviews if something goes wrong. If a guest has a bad experience, be prepared to offer a discount or refund as a way of making it right. If they post a negative review, be prepared to respond promptly and professionally to address their concerns.

7) Not being flexible with check-in and check-out times

Get prepared to get flexible when it comes to the check-in and check-out times. Guests need to know when they can enter and exit the property and it's best if you can be flexible with these times. That is a must.

By not being flexible, your guests may feel restricted or inconvenienced. They might have to wait for their room to become available or have to rush out of their room when their checkout time arrives.

By being flexible and accommodating, you can provide a much better experience for your guests.

Another classic mistake you should avoid as an Airbnb host is not offering enough amenities. People come to Airbnb expecting certain amenities like Wi-Fi, TV, linens, towels, toiletries, and kitchen supplies. Have them ready or brace for the reviews.

Stick with the basic amenities like Wi-Fi and kitchen supplies while leaving some wiggle room in case renters ask for something specific. Oh and take the nine seconds it takes to make sure all amenities you list actually work as expected.

On a very personal note, do not ever overcharge for your rental. While you want to get a good rate for your rental, setting prices too high can dissuade potential renters from renting from you.

Not acceptable.

8) Not providing basic amenities

Failing to provide basic amenities can be a big mistake for Airbnb hosts. Guests expect certain items to be provided in the listing, such as fresh towels and linens, basic toiletries, and kitchen supplies.

Failing to provide these items will leave your guests feeling like they haven't gotten their money's worth and could negatively impact your reviews.

Be sure to include a list of all amenities you provide in your listing, so that guests know what to expect when they arrive.

Restock any items that are used or run out during a guest's stay. Taking the time to provide basic amenities will help ensure your guests have an enjoyable stay.

To get to the highest levels quickly, create checklists of cleaning tasks and instructions for other maintenance activities that need to be done between bookings.

9) Not being responsive to guests' questions

To rise in the ranks as a host, you cannot ignore guests' questions. Your listing, house rules, and other information are now clearly outlined so that that should all be in writing and not up for interpretation.

On the fly requests should be answered asap.

By the way, if one guest has a question, chances are others will have the same one so it's best to answer quickly and thoroughly. And then to include that info in the house manual.

This is a great one. Consider creating a FAQ page on your Airbnb listing that answers common questions that your guests may have. This can help save time and provide a great resource for your guests.

By being proactive and responsive to your guests' questions, you can ensure that they have a smooth and stress-free experience while staying at your Airbnb listing.

10) Not following up after their stay

It's important to make sure you follow up with your guests after they leave. This can be done by sending them a thank you message, or by checking in on them to see how their stay went. Not only will this help you maintain good relationships with your guests, but it's also a great way to get honest feedback on their stay.

If you don't follow up with your guests after their stay, you could be missing out on valuable feedback that could help you improve your Airbnb hosting experience.

Taking the time to thank your guests for staying with you and asking them for their honest opinion on their stay is a simple way to show your appreciation and demonstrate that you care about their experience. You can also use this as an opportunity to ask them for a review or referral for future guests.

Making sure you follow up after each guest's stay is an important part of being an effective Airbnb host. Not only will this help build better relationships with your guests, but it will also help you create a positive reputation for your Airbnb business. So don't forget to take the time to thank your guests after they leave and ask them for their honest feedback.

Also remember to send out a "Welcome Home" package for returning guests. Include items such as small gifts or coupons for local restaurants, stores, or other attractions near your Airbnb property. This gesture not only shows your appreciation for their loyalty, but also encourages them to come back again in the future.

Another mistake many hosts make is not preparing the property properly before check-in. Even if it seems like a small detail, taking the extra steps to spruce up the place prior to check-in can go a long way in making sure your guests have a comfortable stay. Be sure to check all appliances, clean all surfaces, and stock any necessary amenities such as toiletries, towels, etc. In addition, consider leaving some snacks and refreshments so that your guests don't have to go straight to the grocery store when they arrive.

Finally, remember to check in periodically during a guest's stay to ensure everything is going smoothly.

5 Tips For Taking Perfect Airbnb Photos

Great photos are one of the most important marketing tools for getting more bookings. They can make or break a listing, so it's important to get it right. In this chapter, we'll share five simple tips for taking perfect Airbnb photos so that you can crush it and keep a full book.

With these tips, you'll be able to get professional-looking photos that will make your rental stand out from the competition.

So let's get started!

1) Use a Wide-Angle Lens

When taking photos for Airbnb listings, one of the most important things to keep in mind is to use a wide-angle lens. Without question this is one of the best pieces of advice you will ever get.

Wide-angle lenses allow you to capture more of a room in each photo, which can be crucial when trying to show off the space to potential guests.

Wide-angle lenses also help create an illusion of space by stretching the perspective of a room. This can make small spaces seem bigger and brighter, giving the impression that the room is larger than it actually is.

When choosing a wide-angle lens, look for one with an aperture of at least f/2.8. This will help ensure that your photos are well lit and crisp. Make sure to also experiment with different focal lengths to see which one gives you the best results. If you're looking to really emphasize the size of a room, using a wider focal length like 16mm or 24mm might work better than using something like 50mm.

Additionally, if you're shooting from further away, consider using longer lenses like 85mm or even 200mm to compress the background and make the subject stand out more.

When setting up your shots, don't forget to pay attention to details such as furniture placement and window treatments as these small touches can really make or break a photo. It's also important to make sure that everything is clean and clutter free as this will help give potential guests a good first impression. Again we are totally focused on details.

If possible, try to get some natural light into your shots as this will add depth and dimension to your images.

As a follow up thought, you may want to consider investing in some artificial lighting solutions such as softboxes or LED lights if natural light isn't available.

2) Get the Lighting Right

Lighting can make or break a photo, so it's essential to get it right when taking Airbnb photos. A good rule of thumb is to use natural light whenever possible, as this will make the space look more inviting and create more depth in your photos.

Then again, if there are any features that you want to highlight, then artificial light might be necessary.

When using natural light, try to position your camera so that the windows are behind the lens. This will fill the space with soft and even lighting. If the space has multiple windows, you can also experiment with different angles to get the most out of the natural light.

If you need to use artificial lighting, you should choose a high-quality LED or CFL bulb that produces soft and even lighting. Avoid using direct light sources, as this can create hard shadows and make the space look overly harsh. No good.

When positioning lights, try to keep them slightly off-center for a more balanced look. You should also experiment with different levels of brightness and intensity to achieve the best results.

Using different shutter speeds and white balance settings can also help to enhance the atmosphere of your photos.

There is only one goal here...photos that sell your location.

3) Use a Tripod

Might sound contrite, but using a tripod is essential for creating the perfect Airbnb photos.

With a tripod, you can take sharper photos and have more control over the composition. This will help you make sure that all of your shots are well composed and look their best.

When choosing a tripod for your Airbnb photos, look for one that has adjustable legs and is lightweight. This way, you can easily move the tripod around to get the best angles for your photos.

Finally, when taking your photos with a tripod, make sure to keep the camera steady and level. This will ensure that your photos come out looking sharp and professional.

As an added bonus, using a tripod will also make it much easier to take time-lapse or slow motion videos. You'll also find that it's important to experiment with different angles in order to create interesting photos.

Try photographing the same space from different vantage points in order to capture its beauty. If possible, try shooting your photographs during different times of day as well so that you can see how the light changes the room's mood.

Natural Light: Natural light is key when taking Airbnb photos. Make sure to turn on all the lights in the room and open up any curtains or blinds so that the room is full of light. The more natural light you can use, the better your photos will turn out.

Experiment With Props: Adding props to your photos can give them a unique edge. Try adding furniture pieces like rugs or plants in order to add interest and texture to the photo.

4) Shoot in RAW Format

When it comes to taking great Airbnb photos, one of the most important steps is shooting in RAW format. Shooting in RAW gives you the highest quality images and the most flexibility when it comes to post-processing your images. RAW images contain all the original data that the camera captures, allowing you to make adjustments to your images without any degradation of quality.

When shooting with a digital camera, make sure to set your camera to shoot in RAW format instead of JPEG. You may also need to install a photo editor that supports RAW files such as Adobe Lightroom.

By shooting in RAW format, you'll ensure that you have the highest quality images for your Airbnb listing.

Second, take multiple shots from different angles: Even if you think you got the perfect shot from one angle, take multiple shots from different angles so that you can choose the best one later on.

Also consider taking some shots from unexpected angles such as low-angle shots or close-up shots to show more detail.

Once you've taken all your photos, use editing software such as Adobe Lightroom or Photoshop to touch up the images.

5) Use Professional Editing Software

I know we're getting a little nerdy here, but guess what...I want and demand your success so I want you to know these elements. That is exactly why your photos are so valuable.

When it comes to creating the perfect Airbnb photos, professional editing software can be a game-changer. After you've taken your shots, use an editing program like Photoshop or Lightroom to make any necessary adjustments to contrast, brightness, and color.

This will help you create clean, professional looking images that will attract potential renters. If you don't have any experience with these types of software, there are plenty of tutorials online that can teach you the basics. Just head over to YouTube and fish around.

Once you learn the ropes, you'll be able to create stunning images that are sure to make your Airbnb stand out.

You're Going To Crush It On Airbnb Here's How I Know

Story 5

https://www.starterstory.com/stories/how-i-bootstrapped-an-airbnb-management-service-to-35k-month

Airbnb Listing Tips: How to Create the Perfect Listing That Will Stand Out From the Crowd

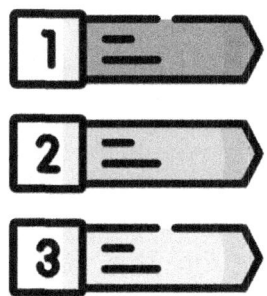

Okay we're getting into it now, folks.

Creating a successful Airbnb listing can feel overwhelming, but it doesn't have to be. With the right guidance and the right tips, you can craft the perfect Airbnb listing that will make your rental stand out from the crowd and attract more potential guests.

So let's then, walk through some of the most important steps and considerations when creating the perfect Airbnb listing. I's hoping at this point that you realize the importance of that in combination with those amazing photos you just learned how to take.

The headline

As a former Madison Avenue Copywriter and Creative Director, I am here to tell you without hesitation that the headline of your Airbnb listing is one of the most important elements that you need to get right.

That new headline is the first thing potential guests will read and it should be super catchy and creative enough to draw their attention and make them want to learn more. I want you to understand that creating one that is memorable could easily set your property up for non stop bookings.

Your headline should include the type of accommodation, the location, and any special features or amenities you are offering. And trust me on this one, getting creative and memorable in your headline is what we are striving for here.

Make sure to use keywords in your description so your listing shows up in search results and ensure that you're one million percent honest in your headline so you don't create false expectations for guests.

In the body of your text, emphasize the unique benefits of staying at your Airbnb rather than simply providing facts and figures about it. Your headline pulls people into those amazing new shots you've just taken so include pictures throughout your post, since pictures will always do a far better job at conveying what your rental looks like than words alone ever could.

We are looking to use our new headline to so up in search results and then motivate those interested to look at our images.

This is where the money is made.

If you are really ready to step up your game, don't forget to mention local attractions, amenities and activities that guests may find interesting during their stay.

It is very important that you sure you include your cancellation policy in order to give potential guests peace of mind when making their decision.

Finally, finish with a strong and compelling call-to-action inviting guests to book now while they still have the chance.

The price

Ah yes, the insider stuff you really need to know. Buckle in for this.

One of the most important elements of creating a successful Airbnb listing is setting a competitive price. You want to make sure that your guests are getting a good value for their money and that you're not pricing yourself out of the market.

And let me make one thing beyond clear, you never ever want to overprice your properties...it is a recipe for disaster that you will not recover from.

The best way to determine a competitive price is to look at similar listings in your area and compare them to yours. Take into account the size of your listing, the amenities you offer, and any additional costs you may have (such as cleaning fees).

It's also important to consider seasonal rates when setting your price. If you're in a vacation destination, you may want to adjust your prices according to the season. This way, you can capitalize on the higher demand during peak travel times.

You should also be aware of any fees that Airbnb might charge you, such as service fees and occupancy taxes. On average, expect to be paying about 14.5% in fees to Airbnb.

Those fees are used to cover things like:

- Customer support
- Marketing via Google and social media
- Protection for hosts and their properties
- Inbox and message center to communicate with guests
- Educational resources for hosts

Finally, make sure that you keep an eye on your prices over time. This one is a biggie. You have to stay on top of this.

Adjusting your prices regularly can help you stay competitive and ensure that your listing remains profitable. And as I have already said, stand ready to offer discounts or free stays to attract more bookings and generate more revenue and more reviews...especially as you just start out.

Super hosts quickly discover that offering discounts or special deals will go far to encourage travelers to book longer stays or commit to booking with you over competitors.

Oh yes, and never forget to highlight your amenities...anything that sets your stay apart.

The amenities

Speaking of amenities, when creating your Airbnb listing, it is important to consider the amenities that you can offer your guests. This is a great way to make your listing stand out from the competition.

As a rule of thumb, the more unique and inviting your amenities, the more guests will gravitate to you know who.

Your amenities should be tailored to the type of guest you are looking to attract and should be carefully selected to provide an enjoyable stay.

The types of amenities that you can include will vary depending on your property, but some examples are:

-A fully equipped kitchen with utensils and cookware
-Complimentary toiletries such as shampoo, conditioner, and body wash
-High-speed internet access
-Cable or satellite television
-Spacious living areas
-Comfortable bedrooms with fresh linens
-Heating and air conditioning
-Outdoor recreational areas such as a pool, patio, or deck

Make sure to list all of your amenities in your listing so that potential guests can see what they can expect when they book your Airbnb. Surprising guests in a bad way will not go well.

As in ever.

So don't do it.

Be sure to keep in mind that some amenities may require additional fees, so make sure to mention this in your listing as well. With these tips in mind, you can easily create a perfect Airbnb listing with all the necessary amenities.

Highlighting unique features and details about your space can help draw more attention to your listing. Furthermore, providing accurate information about your location, check-in process, rules, and nearby attractions can help ensure that guests feel comfortable during their stay.

Go the extra mile and make a link to your house manual available to anyone interested. Make like easy for guests always.

White glove everything you do from here on.

It is super important for you to remember to respond quickly to inquiries and review requests, as this can leave a positive impression on potential renters.

Your cancellation policy

Please lean into this content as this is one of those elements of your new business that you absolutely have to nail.

Having a clear cancellation policy is a huge part of running a successful Airbnb listing. Plain and simple. You want to make sure you are protecting yourself, while also being respectful to guests who may need to cancel their reservation.

First and foremost, decide what kind of cancellation policy you will have.

Airbnb offers three different policies to choose from: flexible, moderate, and strict.

A flexible policy allows for full refunds up to 1 week before check-in, and provides partial refunds after that. A moderate policy allows for full refunds up to 5 days before check-in, and provides partial refunds after that. A strict policy does not provide any refunds unless the guest has an extreme circumstance such as a death in the family or serious illness.

Next, be sure to clearly communicate your policy with potential guests. You should include the cancellation policy in your listing, as well as in any follow up communication you have with the guest. You should also be sure to explain any fees associated with canceling a reservation.

Finally, you should review your policy every so often to make sure it is still appropriate for your listing. I hope you're getting the sense that following up with all of your materials is a big way for you to get profitable very quickly.

Creating a clear cancellation policy is an important part of running a successful Airbnb listing. Being transparent with your guests and making sure they understand your policy will help ensure that they have a positive experience when staying at your property.

Additionally, if you are offering amenities like early check-in or late checkout, be sure to specify how this works in advance. Include details on how early guests can arrive and how late they can stay - having a clear set of rules makes it easier for both you and the guest.

Another way to stand out from other listings is to offer additional services like bike rentals or airport pickup. This can be a great way to add value and create a unique experience for your guests. You are now always looking for ways to separate yourself from everyone else.

Location, Location, And Location

When writing your Airbnb listing, one of the most important factors to consider is the location.

Your potential guests will want to know exactly where the property is located and what kind of area they can expect to stay in so it is now up to you to include a detailed description of its surroundings.

Include nearby attractions, restaurants, shops, parks, transportation options, and more. The more details you can provide, the better informed guests will be about the area.

Be sure to mention any unique features about the location. Is it close to the beach or a popular tourist spot? Is it in a quiet neighborhood? Is it easy to access public transportation? Be sure to point these features out so that guests can make an informed decision about whether the area suits their needs.

Finally, you'll want to include some pictures or videos of the area. Visuals are a great way to showcase your property's location and give potential guests an idea of what they can expect when they arrive.

You can also use Google Maps or other online mapping tools to provide a virtual tour of the area so that guests can get a better sense of the area before booking.

As you now know, adding reviews from previous guests who have stayed at your property is the best way for you to create credibility and trust with potential customers.

The reviews from others who have already had a positive experience with your rental to help reassure them that their vacation rental is worth investing in. This is how Amazon became Amazon...reviews.

In addition to all of this information, providing a comprehensive list of amenities included with the rental can really help set expectations with potential customers. This list should include all available amenities such as appliances, furniture, linens, toiletries, kitchenware, etc., so that there are no surprises on arrival day.

House Rules

Your house rules should let guests know what you expect from them, as well as provide the rules for their stay in your home. Here are some tips for writing clear and concise house rules:

1. Be Respectful: Let your guests know that respect is an important part of their stay in your home. This includes respecting both your property and the privacy of other guests.
2. No Smoking: If you don't allow smoking in your home, make sure to mention this in your house rules.
3. Clean Up After Yourself: Let your guests know that they are expected to clean up after themselves and dispose of any trash properly.
4. Quiet Hours: If you want to enforce a particular quiet time, such as after 10 pm, be sure to include it in your house rules.
5. Check-In/Check-Out Times: Include the check-in and check-out times in your house rules so that guests know when they need to arrive and depart.
6. Pets: If you allow pets in your home, make sure to include any specific pet rules in your house rules.

7. Guests: Let your guests know how many people are allowed in the home at any given time and if visitors or additional guests are allowed.

8. Kitchen: If you have kitchen rules such as not using certain appliances or eating food in the bedrooms, include these in your house rules.

Write your rules so that your guests know precisely what is expected of them in their stay in your home. It's also important to make sure that you communicate any changes to your house rules with guests prior to their arrival so that they are aware of the rules before they enter your property.

Here's a total pro tip at this point...always keep records of any conversations you have had with guests about the house rules. This will come into play if there are any uncomfortabilities during and after they stay, Keeping communication is a must, make sure you make it a priority.

Additionally, if there are any fees associated with breaking the house rules (for example, extra cleaning fees), make sure to state this clearly in your listing and in your house manual.

5 Powerful Ways to Boost Your Airbnb Search Rankings

What you are about to learn in this chapter will change your financial life if you take these thoughts and put them to use.

That agreed to, let's cover five simple but crazy powerful tips that you can use to boost your Airbnb search rankings to get you more bookings.

From leveraging customer reviews to optimizing your listing images, it's time you learn how to improve your visibility and attract more guests.

1) Optimize your photos

When it comes to increasing your Airbnb search rankings, optimizing your photos is one of the most important things you can do. And having read this book, you will.

Your killer photos are the first thing guests will see when they look at your listing, so they should be clear and high quality.

When uploading photos, make sure you use captions to describe each one. This is huge. This will help potential guests understand what they're seeing, and it also helps boost your listing's search engine rankings.

Save your images on your computer and name them using long tail keywords about your property and this will do wonders for you getting found not just on Airbnb but possibly on Google as well and that is when happiness happens.

Look at what your competitors are showing up for in terms of search and simply use those terms to name your locations.

"Airbnb near O'Hare."

"Airbnb closely to Wall Street"

"Airbnb with pool in downtown Sacramento."

Do your research and find the keywords that you will kill to rank for and then name your images with those keywords.

Bingo bango, you start ranking.

Finally, and this one is something that will set you apart on day 1. Don't forget to upload videos of your location.

Videos go the extra mile and showcase your property and give guests a better feel for what they can expect during their stay.

TikTok has exploded with local rental properties all based on zip codes.

Embrace it.

Take out that iPhone and get busy shooting video and needless to say you now know how to name them as they sit on your desktop waiting to be uploaded to almighty Airbnb.

I love it when a plan comes together, don't you?

2) Use the right keywords

Using the right keywords is one of the most important things you can do to boost your Airbnb search rankings. When people search for accommodation on Airbnb, they type in specific keywords that describe what they're looking for.

You want to be showing up for as many unique keywords as possible so by using the right keywords in your Airbnb listing, you will increase your chances of showing up in the search results. And that you can bank on.

Start by making a list of all the relevant words and phrases associated with your Airbnb property. This includes details about the location, amenities, activities, and attractions in the area. For example, if your property is located near a beach, include keywords such as "beach", "ocean view", "surfing", etc.

You should also consider the type of traveler who might stay in your property. If your home caters to families, then include keywords such as "family-friendly", "kids welcome", etc. The more specific you can be when it comes to the keywords you use, the better.

When you're done making your list of keywords, make sure to incorporate them into your listing description. Keep in mind that Airbnb is constantly changing their search algorithm, so it's important to update your keywords regularly to stay ahead of the competition.

Hey where have you heard that before?

3) Keep your calendar up to date

Having an up-to-date calendar on your Airbnb listing is essential for attracting potential guests.

The more availability you have, the more likely you are to get bookings. It is important to be as transparent as possible in terms of when your space is available so that potential guests can plan accordingly. You can adjust your calendar as needed, but be sure to update it regularly so that potential guests know what to expect. Always.

If you have last minute cancellations or changes, make sure to update your calendar so guests can book accordingly. You can also adjust the settings of your calendar to allow for last-minute bookings and adjust rates accordingly.

Stay organized and proactive with your calendar. Make sure you have enough time to prepare your space for guests and that you're not overbooking yourself.

Take advantage of technology to streamline the process, such as using booking automation software, which can help you manage bookings and keep your calendar up to date.

Ask 100 Airbnb hosts which calendar is best and 99 of those great peeps will tell you

that iCal syncs with Google calendar.

So there's that.

4) Respond quickly to inquiries

Being prompt in responding to inquiries is essential for boosting your Airbnb search rankings. If guests don't hear back from you quickly, they may assume that you're not available or reliable. This could lead to them skipping over your listing.

Human beings have the attention span of a toddler, so deal with it and harness it.

To maximize the chances of a potential guest booking with you, respond to their inquiries within 4 hours, if possible. I've heard other people talk about 24 hour, but that's insane in this age of immediacy. So four hours max, one hour if you want to become a big deal.

Make sure to use friendly and professional language when responding. You should also provide all the information they need to make a decision. If you have an automated response system, you can customize it so that it responds quickly and answers their questions.

Oh and let's be clear about one thing here, communication doesn't just stop at the initial inquiry. If you keep in touch with your guests throughout their stay, they're way more likely to leave a positive review afterwards, which will further boost your Airbnb search rankings.

Constantly be asking yourself if you were staying at an Airbnb what would you like to see? What would lead you to breaking out that new pen for that 5 star review?

5) Get positive reviews

Ah yes, the Airbnb holy grail. Reviews.

When it comes to increasing your Airbnb search rankings, getting positive reviews is it.

Reviews help potential guests understand the quality of your property and the level of service they can expect. They also give you a better chance of appearing higher up in the search rankings.

You must never ever stop encouraging guests to leave reviews by offering them a discount or other incentive for doing so.

Follow up with guests after their stay and ask if they had a pleasant experience and if they'd be willing to leave a review. If a guest had a less-than-satisfactory stay, try to resolve any issues that may have occurred so that they can still leave a positive review.

You can also take the initiative and reach out to past guests to solicit reviews. Make sure you reach out at the right time and explain why you're asking for a review in a polite and friendly way.

Finally, when you get positive reviews, share them everywhere, even to previous guests.

Part of your every day now will be to encourage happy customers to post their reviews on social media platforms and use them on your website or other marketing materials because what someone says about you is nine zillion times more effective than anything you say about yourself.

Let me right ahead and say that getting positive reviews will increase your Airbnb search rankings and boost your visibility to potential guests. Take advantage of all the tips mentioned above, and start leveraging reviews to your advantage.

You're Going To Crush It On Airbnb Here's How I Know

Story 6

https://www.escapeyourdeskjob.com/evans-airbnb-story/

How to guarantee 5 star Airbnb reviews

Ah, yes. The 5 star review...and all that they will do for you. As of yesterday, the 5 star gems are your primary focus for each and every guest you have from now until the end of time.

And guess what, it is entirely possible to guarantee 5 star reviews for your Airbnb.

So let's discuss the best practices for ensuring your guests have a great experience, and how to turn that into positive reviews.

1) The importance of reviews

Reviews are a vitally important part of the Airbnb experience, as they provide potential guests with valuable insight into what it's like to stay in a particular rental. Good reviews can make or break your Airbnb business, so it's essential to get as many 5-star ratings as possible.

A good review means more bookings and more money for you. Reviews are also an indication of how well you manage your property and how you interact with guests.

It's important to understand that if you get bad reviews, potential guests may avoid staying at your property. But there are ways to deal with them and we will get to that.

The key to getting great reviews is to ensure that your guests have an above average experience at each and every step of the way with your guests and this certainly includes all of the communication you have with them right out of the gate.

You need to be on top of all the little details such as providing beautifully clean and super comfortable accommodation, being constantly available to answer any and all questions & concerns and you absolutely need to be offering white glove hospitality.

You must listen to what your guests have to say and address any issues they may have during their stay. Let them know that you appreciate their feedback and strive to make their stay as enjoyable as possible.

Keep communication open and honest throughout the rental process, so they can feel comfortable giving you their honest feedback. Make sure your description accurately portrays the rental and its amenities - never overstate or understate anything - so there won't be any surprises when they arrive.

And just so we remember what we have talked about in previous chapters, have a plan for your house rules, your house manual, and a possible welcome gift for them when they initially arrive,

And when you have over-delivered to your guests, never forget to ask them to leave that all-important review after their stay! Most people are happy to help out, but it's easy to forget when life gets busy.

Don't ever be afraid to politely remind them or offer incentives for leaving an honest review - a few kind words from you could go a long way!

If you have done everything you possibly can for them along each step of the way, there is no harm in asking for that review to be five stars...remind them how much that 5 star review will help you and your business.

2) How to get 5 star reviews

Oh, the clarity of it all is stunning. You now know that getting your five-star reviews on Airbnb is essential. Not only do high ratings attract more guests, but they also give a boost of confidence to potential customers. And they will lift you in your local search rankings...all of which are good news for you.

Here are some of the best tips for getting five-star reviews from your guests.

1. Provide an ultra comfortable experience for them nonstop during their stay. Focus on the details, like providing extra toiletries, quality linens, good lighting and a clean space. Make sure that you are available to answer any questions they may have.
2. Be as proactive as possible: Reach out to your guests before they arrive with a welcome message, a reminder about check-in instructions, or a helpful suggestion about

local attractions. Check in with them periodically during their stay to make sure that they have all that they need. (So few hosts will ever do this one thing...and you, having read this...will make it mandatory, The instant feedback they give you, good and bad, is invaluable for all the next guests you serve,

3. Be ultra flexible: Guests really appreciate it if you are accommodating to their requests, such as early check-in or late checkout. Even offering small perks like discounts or freebies can be a great way to show your appreciation.

4. Communicate often: Communicate with your guests throughout the entire stay – from check-in to checkout. If there are any problems, address them immediately and take steps to rectify them.

5. Leave feedback: After the stay has ended, leave a positive review for your guests so that future hosts can see how pleasant it was to have them as tenants. You can also use this opportunity to thank them for staying with you.

Don't ever forget to put yourself in your guest's shoes - what would you want from a host? It's important to be communicative, attentive and professional at all times.

3) What to do if you don't get a 5 star review

Guess what. No matter how much you put into your hosting efforts, unfortunately not all reviews will be positive, and if you don't get a 5-star review, it can be disheartening. Is that fair? Is life fair? Who knows.

The first thing when you get your first less-then-stellar review is to take a deep breath and step back.

It's human nature to get defensive when receiving negative feedback, but it's more important to remember that not every guest is going to have the same experience. Instead of getting defensive or hostile, take a moment to review the feedback carefully and consider what may have gone wrong.

Once you have done that, it's time to reach out to the guest who left the review. Acknowledge their feedback and apologize for any issues that may have been caused by your accommodation or service. Ask them if there is anything you could do to make their stay better or if there is anything else you can do to help.

Your goal here is to win them back. And in all honesty that is not difficult to do.

Take the feedback you got in that review to constantly improve your Airbnb business. Use it as a guide to ways that you could be doing better, Because you can always be doing better for guests. Always.

Keep a record of your improvements so that other guests can see that you are taking their feedback seriously and actively striving to make your accommodation better.

Take the time to respond to negative reviews and/or comments in a professional manner, address the issues raised, and actively implement improvements, then you can turn a bad review into something positive. "We acknowledge that the water pressure was low during your stay with us, and we immediately fixed that issue and we'd love to welcome you back,"

You can demonstrate to potential guests that you are open to feedback, willing to work with them, and committed to providing the best possible experience.

This gives guests peace of mind that you value their opinions (which is so important) and that you are willing to do anything it takes to exceed their expectations. In addition, it shows future guests that you take customer service seriously and have a desire to continually improve.

Automating Your Airbnb Business

At some point on your Airbnb journey, you may feel overwhelmed with all the tasks that need to be done. If so, you're not alone!

One way to solve all of that craziness is automation. Airbnb automation is one of the best ways to streamline your Airbnb business and make it as efficient as possible. And for those of you out there afraid of technology, get over it. Honestly, how bad do you really want this passive lifestyle?

This chapter is about automating your Airbnb business, including the best automation tools, how to use them effectively, and the benefits they will provide to enable you to start making real money and endless bookings easily.

Get ready to be running a well-oiled machine.

Define Your Processes

The key to automating your Airbnb business is to completely define and outline your processes.

Before you can start automating, you need to have a clear plan of how your business should operate. This involves outlining exactly what tasks will be handled, when they will be done, and who will do them. You have to know where you need the most, that is where you will focus when it comes to all of your Airbnb software options.

And there are some great options out there.

Start by considering software that is related to listing management, guest communication, bookings, payments, cleaning, maintenance, etc.

Yeah, that's a cool list. And it is quite important for you to decide which ones can be automated and which ones require manual intervention.

On a personal note, I am of the belief that you should be doing every single thing by hand when you first start. Then you will discover where you need the automated help most.

Once you have your processes defined, create a plan for how each process should work. Write down all the details, including who is responsible for each task, what technology or software will be used to support the process, how often it needs to be done, and any other pertinent information.

Sounds ultra simplistic, but by having all these details in writing, you can ensure that your processes run smoothly and efficiently. You can also use this plan to look for areas where automation might help improve your operations. Remember that you are always looking for roads to improvement. Endlessly.

Here's a perfect example...let's say you want to automate your bookings.

If that is where you need the help most, you can breathe as there are plenty of software solutions available that allow you to integrate with third-party platforms such as Airbnb and HomeAway.

These tools allow you to automate many aspects of managing listings, such as pricing changes, marketing campaigns, and reservation confirmations.

You can also automate guest communications with email templates and automated messages sent via SMS or other messaging systems. You can also set up automation rules to remind guests of upcoming check-in dates or send helpful tips before they arrive.

Finally, you may also want to invest in automation technologies like robotic cleaners or automated locks that make check-in and checkout simpler for both guests and property owners.

Set Up Auto-Responders

Auto-responders are a great way to automate your Airbnb business. This can help you save time, money, and energy. An auto-responder is a computer program that automatically responds to emails, inquiries, and requests.

And for some of the strongest and wealthiest super hosts on Airbnb, they are a must,

With an auto-responder, you can quickly reply to inquiries, confirmations, and messages from guests. This saves you the hassle of manually responding to each message. It also helps make sure that all messages are responded to in a timely manner.

When setting up an auto-responder for your Airbnb business, there are a few things you should consider. First, think about the type of message you want to send. Will it be a welcome message? A confirmation of reservation? Or something else? Make sure the message is polite and professional. Have someone besides you read everything because once messages are loaded into an autoresponder they cannot be stopped until you stop them.

Automation has an ugly side in the wrong hands. Oh the stories I could tell you right now, My advice is be terribly careful with the messages you load into your autoresponders.

Next, decide how often the auto-responder will send out messages. You may want to set up the auto-responder to respond instantly, or set it to wait a certain number of hours before responding.

Consider how often you'd like to receive messages from the auto-responder.

Finally, make sure you test your auto-responder and make sure it's working correctly. You don't want to have any issues with the auto-responder sending out inaccurate messages or having problems with the setup.

By setting up an auto-responder, you can save yourself time and energy while providing a great service to your guests.

So we've covered autoresponders. So check that box.

In addition to auto-responders, there are a ton of other tools that can help automate your Airbnb business. For example, you can use online payment services such as PayPal or Stripe to collect payments from customers securely and efficiently.

Additionally, listing sites such as VRBO or HomeAway allow hosts to list their properties online and manage their bookings easily.

Finally, automated scheduling tools such as ScheduleOnce or Calendly can help streamline the booking process. These tools allow hosts to coordinate check-ins and checkouts without the need for manual scheduling.

They also make it easy to communicate with guests, ensuring that everyone has access to the right information at the right time. These automated tools can significantly reduce manual work for hosts and free them up to focus on other aspects of their Airbnb businesses.

As a final note here.... start by doing it all yourself and you will determine in real time where you need the automated help. But start by getting those hands of yours on every piece of your new hosting business. Do that for me.

Use a Property Management Software

Property management software can dramatically help you take your Airbnb business to the next level. With this type of sophisticated software, you will be able to streamline and automate your operations, saving you time and money. It is also a great way to manage your listings, guests, bookings, payments, and other details related to your Airbnb business.

When selecting property management software for your Airbnb business, look for one that provides features such as automatic payments, automated messages, calendar and availability sync, marketing automation, and access to analytics.

At the end of the day, want to easily keep track of your business's performance and make adjustments as needed.

The goal is for the right software to turn you into a ninja. And it most certainly will.

Another great feature of property management software is its ability to customize your pricing based on the demand of your listing. Which is massive.

This ensures that you are maximizing your profits while also providing competitive prices.

Oh this gets even better when you come to realize that some property management software can also provide you with automated reports that can help you track how successful your listing is doing. How nice would that be over a glass of Pinot at the end of your day?

Plain and simple: property management software can greatly reduce the workload of running an Airbnb business and help you run it far more efficiently.

By the way, always assume that your competitors are already at the software stage. So once you get to it, you need to blaze past them.

And you will.

Hire a Virtual Assistant

I know that there is an incredible pull when it comes to automation inside of your new hosting business. So this next suggestion may seem to come from left field…but it doesn't.

Hiring a virtual assistant is a great way to streamline tasks. A virtual assistant can help you manage the day-to-day operations of your Airbnb business, freeing up more time for you to focus on other aspects of running a successful business.

For those living under a rock, a virtual assistant is someone in a remote country like The Philippines, India or many of the eastern European block countries and many other corners of the globe. These people will do the day to day tasks that you may be too busy to do.

A virtual assistant can do everything from managing guest communications to helping with check-in and check-out. They can also manage all the logistics and provide support with customer service issues.

By hiring a virtual assistant, you can outsource many of the tedious tasks associated with running an Airbnb business, allowing you to focus on more important areas.

I have been using virtual assistants for the past 12 years and when it comes to this part of your arsenal, trust me when I tell you that finding the right VA is pure gold…because not all of them are pure gold.

That's me winking at you through a book.

When it comes to finding the right virtual assistant for your business, there are many online services that you can use to find qualified candidates. Most of these services have reviews from past customers which can help you decide who to hire.

When choosing a virtual assistant, be sure to ask them questions about their experience and skills so that you can ensure that they have the right qualifications for the job.

For those of you with short attention spans (like me) here is a list of what Google considers to be the best places to search for VAs at the time of the writing of this book.

Best Virtual Assistant Services of 2023

- Best Overall: Time etc.
- Best for Solopreneurs: Prialto
- Best for Small Businesses: Upwork
- Best for On-Demand Tasks: Fancy Hands
- Best for Specialized VAs: Belay
- Best for Rush Projects: Magic
- Best Service Guarantee: Wood Bows

And of course there is always Fiverr.com where all tasks used to be $5. But now it is the wild wild west in terms of pricing and quality.

Once you have hired a virtual assistant, make sure that you provide them with detailed instructions and guidelines so that they understand exactly what is expected of them. This will help ensure that your virtual assistant is productive and efficient.

Let me stop the flow here and say one thing: unless you are incredibly specific with virtual assistants you will be let down. Guaranteed. So take the time upfront to bullet point precisely what you expect and in what time frame.

More Automation Equals More Bookings

Oh, let's move it all up a notch in terms of the customer experience when it comes to the automations available to you and your hosting business.

Time To Use a chatbot

Chatbots are a great way to automate your Airbnb messaging. And they can be super easy to build with some of the new software options out there that compete with Manychat options.

A killer chatbot will quickly and easily answer common questions from guests and help you manage incoming messages more efficiently. It runs 24/7 and gives immediate answers to the typical questions guests will always have,

Personally, I love chatbots. But they have to be crafted correctly or you are going to upset guests.

You can even program your chatbot to greet guests when they message you and respond with predetermined answers based on the questions they ask which is a nice feature.

You can also have the bot be ready to deliver the latest version of the house manual and the house rules.

But where it could shine is when you load your new bot with all the local amenities. "Best Italian Food". "Place for dinner with kids." "Bowling alley."

Think about all of things you would ask your host. And load them into a chatbot. Hell, you don't even need a hosting account for the best bots.

But you can make sure that they answer 90% of all the questions

Chatbots can save you time by automating basic communication tasks. By automating some of the most frequently asked questions, like check-in times and directions, you won't have to spend time writing individual responses to each guest.

And yes, you can use chatbots to send out reminders or promotional messages to potential or past guests.

To use a chatbot, you'll first need to find a platform that supports chatbot functionality. Many of the popular messaging platforms like Facebook Messenger, Slack, and Telegram offer various integrations with chatbots.

Yet Manychat stands as the leader as we write this.

Once you've found the platform you want to use, you'll need to create the bot's script. This script will define the bot's behavior and how it will respond to different queries.

Automate your listing

Managing a successful Airbnb listing can be a time-consuming task. By automating certain aspects of your listing, you can save time and maximize efficiency.

Here are a few tips for automating your Airbnb listing:

1. Set up a welcome message: Automatically greet your guests when they book a stay at your property by setting up a welcome message. You can include helpful information like the check-in process, Wi-Fi details, and local attractions.
2. Automate your house rules: Make sure all of your guests know the house rules before they arrive. Automate your house rules so that they are sent to each guest who books with you.
3. Set up reminders: Keep in touch with your guests and remind them of important information such as check-out times, payment deadlines, and other policies. Automate reminders so that these messages are sent out automatically, saving you time and energy.
4. Automate cleaning instructions: Streamline the check-in process by sending automated instructions on how to clean the property after each stay.

By automating certain aspects of your listing, you can save yourself time and energy and ensure that every guest has a pleasant experience. Taking advantage of these automation tools can help you manage your Airbnb listing more efficiently and effectively.

Automate your calendar

One of the most time-consuming parts of managing an Airbnb rental is keeping up with your calendar. You have to make sure you stay on top of bookings, respond to inquiries, and adjust the availability of your listings.

Your calendar is front and center so treat it as such starting now.

Fortunately, there are tools available that can help you automate your calendar and take the stress out of keeping up with bookings.

First, you should set up automatic responses to any booking requests. By using automated responses, you can quickly respond to guests and let them know if their booking request has been accepted or rejected. This will save you time because you won't have to manually respond to every request.

Next, you should consider setting up an auto-booking feature. With auto-booking, you can automatically accept bookings when they come in. This will save you time because you don't have to manually check each request.

Finally, you should look into automating your availability settings. By automating your availability, you can ensure that your listing is always available when you want it to be. This can help you maximize your income by filling all available slots quickly.

Use an auto-responder for reviews

Reviews are a great way to ensure your Airbnb is well-maintained and that you're providing a high level of service. Problem is, responding to each review takes a lot of time. To save yourself time, you can set up an auto-responder for reviews.

You already know now that auto-responders are pre-written scripts. Why not set them up to respond to reviews automatically?

You can customize the messages so they sound natural, and include important information about your rental, such as check-in and check-out times.

By using an auto-responder for reviews, you can save time and provide customers with more information about your rental in a timely manner. Plus, you can keep track of all the reviews you've received in one place, allowing you to make sure you're always up to date.

(Yep, there's that staying up to the minute thing again. I'm repeating it because I never want you to forget it as it is one of the best ways to smoke your competitors.)

To get started with setting up an auto-responder for reviews, you'll need to sign up for a third-party service.

Here's what Google thinks when it comes to the top 10 autoresponders out there:

The Best 10 Autoresponder Software

- HubSpot
- GetResponse

- Moosend
- Aweber
- Klaviyo
- Mailchimp
- ConvertKit
- Autopilot

Once you have the software and your script in place, customize the message to reflect your Airbnb's policies and services. Make sure to include any other relevant information that will be helpful to your customers.

The moment it is live, your auto-responder will take care of sending out responses to reviews on your behalf. This will seriously help you save time while still providing customers with the information they need.

You can also respond to reviews that are less than 4 stars instantly once the reviews have been captured.

Automate Your Airbnb Pricing

You're probably starting to realize the enormous potential of having the right software for your hosting business. And it is just wild what you will be able to do...when you are ready for it.

So to whet the whistle even further, let's discuss the best strategies for automating your Airbnb pricing so that you can maximize your income while minimizing your workload. Sound okay to you?

What are the benefits of automated pricing?

When it comes to renting out your space on Airbnb, setting a competitive price can be a time-consuming and stressful task.

That's why many property owners have begun to explore automated pricing solutions.

Automating your Airbnb pricing means that you can set your rental rate according to the market conditions, helping you to maximize your profits while providing a great service to your guests.

Think about that for a moment and allow yourself to get psyched as hell.

Naturally, one of the biggest advantages of automated pricing is that it saves you time and energy. With automated pricing, you don't have to constantly monitor and adjust your prices manually.

Here are some of the best Airbnb pricing software options out there now:

1. Wheelhouse
2. Beyond Pricing
3. Pricelabs
4. AirDNA Recommended Rates
5. Outswitch

The best pricing software will automatically adjust your prices based on specific criteria that you set. This makes it so much easier for you to stay ahead of the competition. A spot I want you in always.

Automated pricing will also help you keep up with trends in your market which is invaluable.

Let's say there's a surge in demand for Airbnb properties in your area, automated pricing can help you adjust your prices accordingly. Can you see how this type of software will instantly give you an edge over other hosts who don't have automated pricing in place?

Finally, and I want this not to go unnoticed: automated pricing is great for customers too! Your guests will benefit from competitively priced listings that they can easily compare and choose from.

Let's be clear as crystal as they say, Automated pricing offers significant benefits for both property owners and customers. It simplifies the process of setting and adjusting rental rates, so you can make sure you're getting the best value for your space.

You know by now that I like to add a PS at the end of chapters...so here's this one.

PS. Automated pricing is that it can help you increase bookings by targeting potential customers more effectively. For instance, some platforms allow you to customize your pricing for different locations or types of guests. Love it.

What are some things to consider when automated pricing?

When considering automated pricing for your Airbnb, there are several important factors to consider.

1. Competition – You want to make sure that you're pricing your Airbnb competitively with other similar listings in the area. Researching what competitors are charging for their listings will help ensure that you're offering a price that is attractive to potential guests.
2. Local market trends – Being aware of the current market trends in your area will help you set the optimal price for your listing. Consider when peak travel times are, as well as other factors such as major events and holidays which may affect prices.

3. Long term vs short term bookings – If you're offering both long-term and short-term bookings, you'll need to take these into account when setting automated pricing. You may need to offer different prices depending on whether your guest is booking a single night or staying for a longer period of time.

4. Your own preferences – As the owner of your Airbnb, you know best what you're comfortable charging for your listing. Make sure to factor in your own personal preferences and goals when setting automated prices for your property.

Take the route that the super hosts have paved and look into the best pricing software when you are ready for it and ensure that you're maximizing your income and setting your Airbnb apart from the competition by offering competitively priced bookings.

How do I get started with automated pricing?

If you're ready to take the plunge and automate your Airbnb pricing, here are some steps to get started.

1. Research other properties. Take a look at what other hosts in your area are charging for their listings. This will give you an idea of where you should start pricing your own rental.

2. Set up dynamic pricing. Dynamic pricing is a type of automated pricing that adjusts your rate based on market demand. This allows you to maximize your profits while still offering competitive rates to your guests. Many software programs offer dynamic pricing capabilities.

3. Consider setting up minimum and maximum prices. This will ensure that you don't go too low or too high with your rates.

4. Set up seasonal pricing. If you plan on taking a break from Airbnb during certain times of year, it's a good idea to set up seasonal pricing that reflects this. For instance, if you plan on taking a break during the winter months, you may want to adjust your prices accordingly.

5. Monitor your progress. Once you've automated your Airbnb pricing, it's important to keep an eye on your results. Make sure you're getting the return on investment you're expecting, and adjust as needed.

As with anything new, there may be bumps along the way when it comes to automating your Airbnb pricing. But if you stay on top of monitoring your performance and make adjustments when necessary, you'll be able to reap the full benefits of automation in no time. It's something that is simply going to happen. Pure and simple.

Get Rid of the Keys: How to Automate Your Airbnb Check-In

At some point in the near future, you may tire of the process of exchanging keys with your Airbnb guests.

It happens. The traditional key exchange process for Airbnb hosts is an inconvenience and can leave you feeling vulnerable.

Luckily, there are now solutions that can help you automate your Airbnb check-in and key exchange process, making it easier and more secure.

So let's see how you can get rid of the keys and automate your Airbnb check-in so you can have more peace of mind.

Why Automate Your Check-In?

Airbnb key exchange can be a hassle for both guests and hosts. It often involves awkward scheduling, long distance coordination, and exchanging physical keys or codes.

By automating your check-in process, you can save time and streamline the experience for all parties involved. Something we always strive for daily.

Automation done at the highest level will also increase security, reduce costs associated with replacing lost keys, and make check-in more reliable. Check, check and check.

Many hosts are already utilizing automated check-in solutions that provide ease of use, convenience, and peace of mind to both guests and hosts. Automation can free up more of your time to focus on other aspects of your business.

For example, you can schedule the check-in process so it's seamless, eliminating the need for staff to be onsite at all times to greet guests. Done to the perfection you will do it at, automated solutions allow for keyless entry, which means you don't have to worry about keeping track of physical keys.

Overall, automating your Airbnb key exchange can help create an effortless guest experience while allowing you to focus on running and growing your business.

You'll no longer need to worry about staying late to meet late arrivals or having to jump in your car to give someone a key! By automating this process, it makes it easy for guests to access their space quickly, securely, and conveniently.

There are several automated solutions out there to choose from depending on your individual needs. Consider researching different options to find the one that best suits you.

Be sure to look into security measures as well, such as two-factor authentication and encryption capabilities. With the right automation solution, you can enjoy a secure and hassle-free Airbnb check-in process

What You'll Need

If you want to automate your Airbnb check-in, there are a few things you'll need. First, you'll need an access control system that can be integrated with your Airbnb listing. This can be a keyless entry system or a smart lock. Second, you'll need to install the access control system at your property.

Depending on the system you choose, this can be done by a professional or a do-it-yourselfer.

Third, you'll need to make sure your access control system is compatible with your Airbnb listing.

Most modern systems are compatible with popular home automation systems, such as Google Home and Amazon Alexa. Finally, you'll need to make sure that the access control system is easy for guests to use, so that they can check in without any hassles.

Once you have all of these components in place, you're ready to start automating your Airbnb check-in process.

The first step is to configure your access control system. Depending on which type of system you've chosen, you may need to program different settings for different users.

For example, if you'd like some guests to be able to enter anytime, while others only during certain times, you'll need to create separate settings for each user. You'll also need to configure your access control system to work with your Airbnb listing.

This will ensure that when someone books your listing, their key code will automatically be sent to them. Additionally, some systems allow you to customize automated messages sent out when someone books or checks out of your property.

Set Up Your Automated Check-In

Setting up an automated check-in for your Airbnb is a great way to save time and make the process simpler for your guests. Automating your check-in process also allows you to keep better track of who is coming and going from your rental property.

The first step to automating your check-in process is to set up an automated welcome message. This message should include instructions on how to enter your property, such as providing the address and any access codes they will need. You can set this up in your Airbnb account or in the app itself.

Next, you should set up an automated key exchange system. You can do this by installing a keypad lock on your door. A keypad lock gives your guests access to the property without you having to be there to give them a physical key. There are many types of keypad locks available that offer varying levels of security.

You can also use a smart lock system to provide your guests with access to the property. Smart locks are connected to the internet and allow you to grant access remotely. This means that even if you aren't present, you can still provide your guests with access to the property at any time.

Finally, you can set up an automated check-out process. This can be done using an automated email system or through the Airbnb app.

An automated check-out process allows you to collect feedback from your guests and helps keep track of when your property has been vacated.

By setting up an automated check-in and check-out process, you'll be able to save time and keep track of who is coming and going from your rental property.

Set Up Your Smart Lock

Setting up your smart lock for automated check-in is easy. All you need is a compatible lock, such as the August Smart Lock Pro, and a compatible Wi-Fi router.

The first step is to install the lock. This should be done according to the instructions that come with your device. After that, you'll need to connect the lock to your Wi-Fi network. You can do this by downloading the app that comes with your lock and following the on-screen instructions.

Once the lock is connected to your Wi-Fi network, you will be able to use the app to set up access codes and schedules.

This allows you to create different codes for different guests so they can access the property during their scheduled stay. You can also use the app to monitor who has accessed the property and when.

It's important to make sure that you secure your system properly. This means setting up strong passwords and enabling two-factor authentication if possible. This will help ensure that only the guests you give access to are able to get in.

By following these steps, you will have everything you need to set up an automated key exchange for your Airbnb rental. Automating this process will save you time and make it easier for your guests to get in and out of your property.

With an automated key exchange, you don't have to worry about being around to greet your guests or handing over physical keys.

You may even be able to offer late check-ins or early check-outs without having to worry about being there yourself. Plus, you won't have to worry about losing physical keys or dealing with other common problems associated with traditional keys.

Another benefit of automation is that it gives you more control over how your guests access the property. You can limit the number of people allowed inside at any given time or restrict them from certain areas within the property. Plus, you can receive notifications whenever someone enters or exits the building.

Finally, automation also gives you peace of mind knowing that your property is always secure and under your control. With an automated key exchange, you don't have to worry about unauthorized entry or other security threats.

Here's what people much smarter than me think when it comes to choosing the best smart locks for your Airbnb property:

Here are some of the Best Airbnb smart locks:

1. August Smart Lock

2. Kwikset
3. Schlage
4. Yale
5. Honeywell
6. Ultraloq
7. Lockly

Test Your System

Once you have set up your automated check-in system and have your smart lock installed, it is important to test your system before you start using it. Testing your system will help ensure that everything is working properly, and will help to make sure that your guests have a smooth check-in process.

First, make sure all the parts are in place. Make sure you've configured the app settings and Wi-Fi correctly, and that all the cables are connected properly. Then test it out yourself by going through the same steps a guest would go through.

Do not nod here. Do it. Your safety is my number one concern and that keyless entry is a very big deal. Please follow through on the testing,

See if you can access the code to unlock the door from the app. Make sure the door opens and closes correctly.

If there are any issues, or if something isn't working as expected, don't hesitate to reach out to customer service for assistance. It's better to address any potential problems before guests arrive than after.

Once you've tested the system, you're ready to start using it for automated check-ins!

Depending on how you've set up your automated key exchange system, your guests may need to follow certain instructions when they first arrive. For example, some systems require guests to first use their phone to generate an access code in order to open the door.

Letting your guests know what they need to do ahead of time will make their check-in process simpler and faster.

Finally, and this is a biggie...I want you to make sure you keep backups of the codes somewhere safe so that you have quick access to them should an emergency occur.

By having a safe backup solution, you'll be able to quickly provide someone with access if needed. With an automated key exchange system in place, key management becomes much easier.

How cool is that? How cool is this whole Airbnb model? I hope you are so excited.

You're Going To Crush It On Airbnb Here's How I Know

Story 7

https://www.reddit.com/r/AirBnB/comments/54na24/how_my_airbnb_hosting_experience_went_or_how_i/

The Complete Guide to Automating Your Airbnb Business

Who here does not yet appreciate the fact that automating your Airbnb business is a great way to streamline operations, save time, and make more money.

Show of hands? Anyone?

In this chapter, I'm about to provide you with a complete guide to automating your Airbnb business. From setting up automated payment processes to using smart home technologies, this guide will show you all the steps you need to take to get your Airbnb business running smoothly.

Introducing IFTTT

IFTTT (If This Then That) is a killer automated web service that allows you to create simple rules or "recipes" that will help you automate your entire Airbnb business.

IFTTT is simple to use and incredibly powerful. It allows you to connect different web applications and services together, making it easy to automate routine tasks and free up your time for more important things. All of this can be used to enable you to dominate the tech side of Airbnb hosting.

Using IFTTT, you can create recipes that are triggered when certain conditions are met.

For example, you could set up a recipe that sends you an email whenever you get a new reservation on Airbnb. You could also create recipes that turn on the lights when someone checks in, post automatic updates on social media, or even send out personalized messages to guests.

Cool, to be sure.

The possibilities are endless and IFTTT makes it easy to get started. All you have to do is sign up for an IFTTT account, set up your recipes, and then let IFTTT take care of the rest.

Once you get your recipes set up, all you need to do is sit back and let IFTTT handle all of your Airbnb automation needs.

Not only does this software allow you to focus on other aspects of running your business, but it also saves you money by automating mundane tasks such as responding to emails, updating listings, and processing payments.

IFTTT is also constantly adding new features and improvements, so you can always be sure that you're getting the most out of this powerful tool. Plus, since IFTTT works with so many other web apps and services, you'll never run out of ideas for how to automate your Airbnb business. From setting up automated emails to posting automatic updates on social media, there's no limit to what you can do with IFTTT.

For those of you serious about making bank as a host, IFTTT is a mandatory.

Setting up your IFTTT account

In order to get started, you'll need to create a simple IFTTT account. So head on over to the IFTTT website and sign up.

Once you've entered your email address and password, you'll be taken to a dashboard. Here you can access the recipes, which are the instructions for setting up specific automations.

Next, you'll need to connect your Airbnb account to IFTTT. To do this, click on "My Services" in the top right corner of the screen.

From there, select "Airbnb" and enter your login credentials.

Once connected, you're ready to start creating recipes for your Airbnb business! You can find pre-made recipes from other users or you can create your own from scratch.

Before you get started, you should spend some time exploring all the possible ways to automate tasks for your Airbnb business.

For example, you could use IFTTT to automatically post your listings to social media whenever you update them. Or you could set up a recipe to remind you to follow up with guests after they book their stay.

You sensing the possibilities here?

Connecting IFTTT to your Airbnb account

Okay, let's move on this because IFTTT is a beast.

In order to get started with IFTTT, you'll need to connect your Airbnb account to the service.

Here's how you can do it:

1. Sign into IFTTT and click on "My Applets" at the top of the page.
2. Next, click on the "+" button to create a new applet.
3. Select "this" on the left side and search for "Airbnb".
4. Select the trigger or action you want to use and follow the instructions to link your Airbnb account to IFTTT.
5. On the right side, select "that" and then choose the action you want to occur after the trigger is triggered. For example, if you want to send an email to guests when their booking request is accepted, you would choose "Email" as the action.
6. Finally, enter all of the necessary information for the action, such as the recipient's email address, and click "Finish" to complete the setup process.

Once you've connected your Airbnb account to IFTTT, you can start creating automated recipes that will save you time and effort while managing your Airbnb business.

For instance, you could create an applet that automatically updates your calendar when a guest books your property, so you don't have to manually update the calendar yourself.

You can also set up notifications to alert you whenever certain events happen in your Airbnb account, such as a guest leaving feedback or a payment being made. With these notifications, you'll always be up-to-date with what's going on in your business.

My goodness...the endless possibilities. You can even set up automatic responses to inquiries so that potential guests receive prompt replies from you.

Creating IFTTT recipes for your Airbnb business

Creating IFTTT recipes is easy and only requires a few steps.

First, you'll need to select an applet from the IFTTT library. Once you've chosen an applet, you'll need to select a trigger and an action. The trigger is the event that triggers the action to occur.

For example, if you want to send out a welcome message when someone books your Airbnb, your trigger would be a new reservation being made. The action is the task that will be performed when the trigger occurs. In this case, the action would be to send a welcome message.

Once you have chosen your trigger and action, you'll need to customize the applet to fit your needs. This involves setting up the details of the trigger and action such as setting the time frame for when the action should occur and entering any required information for the action.

Once you have customized your applet, all that is left to do is test it out to make sure it works as expected. If everything works as expected, then you can save your recipe and start automating your Airbnb business.

Additionally, if you don't find an existing applet that fits your specific needs, you can also create your own custom applets. And super hosts will tell you that this is where the magic happens for them

Simply select "Create" instead of "Discover" in the IFTTT homepage. From there, you'll be able to customize the ingredients and settings in order to create the perfect recipe for your Airbnb business.

Once you have saved your Airbnb recipes, you can sit back and relax knowing that your automated processes are taking care of most of the tedious tasks associated with running your Airbnb business. You will no longer have to worry about remembering to reach out to guests after they book or manually updating calendars; these are just some examples of what can be automated using IFTTT.

Testing and troubleshooting your IFTTT recipes

Read that chapter headline and then read it again 940 times. That's how important the accuracy of them is to me as I present them to you.

It is now mandatory for you to test and retest your IFTTT recipes before you start using them for your Airbnb business. This ensures that everything is running as it should and will help avoid any potential problems down the line.

Automation is beautiful, but if it is running wrong, it could be devastating and I need you to know that.

The first step in testing and troubleshooting your IFTTT recipes is to enable debug mode.

Debug mode allows you to monitor and adjust your recipes in real-time, and helps you identify any potential issues before they become a problem. To enable debug mode, log into your IFTTT account and select "Settings" from the top navigation bar. Then scroll down to the "Debug Mode" section and switch the toggle to "On".

Once you have enabled debug mode, you can start testing your recipes.

Start by manually activating each of your recipes to make sure they are triggering correctly. You can also use the IFTTT "Check Recipe" feature to validate each recipe and receive real-time feedback on its performance.

If you find that your recipes are not working as expected, try editing the recipes to make sure all of the settings are correct. If that doesn't solve the issue, reach out to the IFTTT support team for further assistance. They should be able to help you troubleshoot any issues you are having with your recipes.

Above everything do not launch anything unless you have two green lights on it all.

Going beyond IFTTT with Zapier

Zapier is a powerful automation tool that can be used to streamline your Airbnb business.

With Zapier, you can create automated workflows that connect your Airbnb account to other services.

Let's imagine that you want to create a workflow that will automatically send an SMS message to a customer when a booking is made. You can also use Zapier to trigger emails when bookings are cancelled, or to remind guests of check-in instructions.

Zapier also allows you to connect your Airbnb account to other services such as Slack and Trello. Whether you know right now the power of these software giants, you will.

They are incredibly powerful.

This means that you can set up automated notifications and tasks in these services whenever something happens in your Airbnb account. For example, you can set up notifications in Slack when new bookings come in, or create tasks in Trello when a customer sends an inquiry.

The amount of automation and communication and time saving simply cannot be estimated...it will always come down to how much you want to do on these sites and how willing you are to learn them.

My advice: learn them big time.

Using Zapier can be intimidating at first, but there are plenty of resources available to help you get started. Zapier has an extensive library of tutorials and documentation, as well as helpful customer support staff who can answer any questions you may have.

With some practice, you can easily set up powerful automated workflows for your Airbnb business using Zapier. Additionally, Zapier's free plan offers enough features to get started with automating your Airbnb business.

As your hosting business grows, you can upgrade your plan to access even more advanced features and don't forget that you can always bring in a VA to help you do all of this...just be careful when you give them access to your computer from remote locations.

To make sure that all of your automation settings run smoothly, it's important to regularly review them. Make sure all triggers are configured correctly, and keep an eye out for any problems with the automated flows you've created. Finally, don't forget to occasionally test out the flows manually to make sure everything is working properly.

Automating your Airbnb business with Zapier can save you time and money by allowing you to focus on the aspects of your business that require more attention.

By setting up these automated processes, you'll be able to take back control of your time and spend more time on the activities that will help grow your Airbnb business.

Airbnb hosting in 2023: the pros, the cons, and everything in between

The sharing economy has transformed the travel industry in recent years, and Airbnb has become one of the leading players.

But what does Airbnb hosting look like in 2023 and beyond?

What should you know before deciding to become an Airbnb host? In this chapter, we'll look at the pros, the cons, and everything in between when it comes to hosting through Airbnb in 2023 and way beyond.

From legal considerations to tax implications, we'll cover all the important facts about hosting an Airbnb in 2023.

The future of Airbnb

As one of the leading players in the hospitality industry, Airbnb has changed the way people travel and stay in accommodations. As a result, it has been disrupting the traditional hotel industry since its founding in 2008.

Airbnb is growing exponentially and currently operates in 191 countries, with over 7 million listings. It is predicted that Airbnb will continue to disrupt the hospitality industry even further in the future. In 2023, there will be more opportunities than ever before for people to make money through Airbnb hosting.

Airbnb hosting offers a range of benefits and drawbacks, and it's important to consider these carefully before deciding to become an Airbnb host.

However, with the right preparation, Airbnb hosting can be a lucrative business opportunity.

You ready to explore the pros and cons of hosting on Airbnb in 2023 and get the smartest tips for first-time Airbnb hosts?

The Pros - Hosting on Airbnb in 2023 provides an excellent opportunity for those who want to supplement their income or turn their space into an additional source of income. For example, if you own a house or apartment, you can rent out a room or your entire home when you're away or not using it.

Additionally, Airbnb offers high rates of return when compared to other types of rentals. Hosts typically receive 70-80% of their rental fees from each booking.

The Cons - While Airbnb does offer significant potential for earning income, there are also some downsides to hosting. For example, being an Airbnb host requires some upfront work such as preparing your property for guests and responding promptly to inquiries from potential guests.

Additionally, hosting means having to share your space with strangers, which may not be ideal for some people. Additionally, depending on your local laws and regulations, there may also be tax implications involved in renting out your property.

The benefits of hosting on Airbnb

Airbnb has become one of the most popular ways to earn extra income over the past few years, and with good reason. Hosting on Airbnb offers a number of advantages for those who choose to do so.

First, hosting on Airbnb provides an easy way to make some extra money without having to commit to a long-term rental agreement or any other type of contract. You can choose when and how often you want to list your property, and this flexibility gives you the opportunity to tailor your hosting experience to your own schedule and lifestyle.

Second, Airbnb hosts have access to a global audience of potential renters. This means that you can easily find people from all around the world who are interested in renting your property, potentially leading to higher profits.

Third, Airbnb hosts can also benefit from additional services such as insurance and property management. These services provide added peace of mind when it comes to protecting your investment and ensuring that your guests have a great stay.

Finally, hosting on Airbnb is a great way to connect with people from different cultures and backgrounds. You can meet interesting travelers and get to know more about the world around you, all while making money in the process.

Plus, many travelers are looking for unique experiences, which makes hosting on Airbnb especially appealing since you can offer something no hotel can match.

In addition, hosting on Airbnb typically results in fewer taxes than if you rented through traditional channels such as hotels. This means that you keep more of the earnings for yourself.

Plus, you don't have to worry about collecting taxes from your guests like traditional rentals would require.

Furthermore, there's the chance to gain helpful insights into the local area and its culture. Knowing what guests look for can help shape a better vacation experience for them, which is beneficial for both parties involved.

Overall, hosting on Airbnb in 2023 will come with many advantages, both financially and otherwise. Of course, there are still certain risks involved, but with the right precautions taken, these risks can be minimized. All in all, Airbnb looks set to remain a popular platform for generating supplemental income well into the future.

The drawbacks of hosting on Airbnb

Airbnb hosting isn't always a bed of roses. There are some drawbacks that potential hosts need to be aware of before diving into this exciting opportunity.

First, Airbnb can be a lot of work. Hosts are responsible for advertising and managing their listing, communicating with guests, providing amenities and housekeeping, and responding to complaints. If you don't have the time or the energy to keep up with these demands, it's probably not a good idea to take on an Airbnb.

Second, your home could be damaged. Although Airbnb provides liability insurance to protect hosts, they can't prevent guests from causing damage to the property. That's why it's important to have a set of rules and expectations for guests in your listing, as well as a comprehensive damage deposit policy.

Finally, you may have to pay taxes on your earnings. Depending on where you live, Airbnb income may be subject to local taxes, and you'll need to include your earnings in your annual income tax filing. Make sure you understand the applicable tax laws in your area so you can properly report any income you make from Airbnb hosting.

You should also research zoning restrictions in your city to make sure you're allowed to rent out your space legally.

In addition, you'll want to be aware of safety concerns when hosting through Airbnb. Have clear safety protocols for both yourself and your guests, such as making sure all doors are locked at night, having proper lighting around entrances and exits, having smoke detectors and fire extinguishers installed, etc. You should also screen your guests carefully before allowing them to stay in your space.

Finally, bear in mind that there is no guarantee when it comes to Airbnb hosting. Your property might remain vacant for extended periods of time, especially during times of economic downturn or travel restrictions due to public health concerns.

It's important to be prepared for these scenarios by budgeting carefully and keeping enough savings available just in case. With careful planning and knowledge of the risks involved, however, Airbnb hosting can still be a great way to earn extra money in 2023.

Your New Airbnb Hosting Mindset

If you're considering becoming an Airbnb host, it's so damn important to understand the Airbnb hosting mindset.

Hosting on Airbnb can be a great way to make extra money while providing people with a unique, memorable experience.

Let's Recap Shall We?

When you're getting started as an Airbnb host, it's important to develop the right Airbnb mindset. That means having the proper expectations and understanding of the process.

Here is what you now know to be true and exactly what you are about to act upon:

1. Location – Where is your property located? This can make a big difference in your success as an Airbnb host. The more popular areas, such as cities and beach destinations, tend to have higher demand.
2. Guests – What kind of guests do you want to host? Are you open to hosting families or just solo travelers? Decide which

type of guests you'd like to welcome into your home and make sure to tailor your Airbnb listing accordingly.

3. Amenities – What amenities can you offer? From fully-equipped kitchens to cozy linens, the amenities you provide will play a major role in your success. Make sure to list all the amenities you can provide in your Airbnb listing.

4. Pricing – How much should you charge for a night? Research what other hosts in your area are charging and determine how competitive you want to be with pricing. Be sure to keep costs in mind when setting your prices, as any profits will be offset by cleaning and other expenses.

If you don't have the right Airbnb mindset today, just act as if you do. Fake it till you make it as they say.

What kind of host do you want to be?

So, are you looking to make some extra money by renting out your space on occasion? Or do you want to be a dedicated, full-time Airbnb host? Do you prefer a hands-off approach or would you rather be more involved with your guests?

Having an idea of what type of host you'd like to be will help you decide which hosting strategies and policies to put in place.

Understanding what kind of guests you'd like to attract is also important. Are you looking for more business travelers or more leisure travelers? Do you prefer guests that stay for a few days or a few weeks? Knowing who your ideal guest is will help ensure that the guests you're inviting into your home are compatible with your goals and values as a host.

Finally, decide what type of host you want to be, it's important to consider the level of hospitality and service that you're willing to offer. Are you happy just providing a bed and bathroom for your guests, or do you want to go the extra mile and provide breakfast, snacks, and other amenities?

Understanding your own capabilities will help ensure that you're able to deliver on your promises as a host.

Set Hosting Boundaries

When it comes to setting boundaries for guests, communication is key.

Make sure to clearly outline what is acceptable and unacceptable behavior from guests before they arrive. This can be done through your house rules, or other forms of communication such as messages or emails.

You need to set limits on noise levels and when guests are allowed to be in certain parts of your home. By being clear on these expectations beforehand, it will help prevent any confusion or issues while guests stay at your place.

On the other hand, it's also important to set boundaries for yourself.

As an Airbnb host, you need to understand that hosting is not always a one-way street. It's important to make sure that you're not overextending yourself by providing too much to guests.

Setting boundaries for yourself will help ensure that you don't end up feeling taken advantage of or stressed out by hosting.

Overall, understanding the importance of setting boundaries is a key part of cultivating the right Airbnb mindset.

I'm beyond honored that you have read this far. It's the biggest sign that you will succeed.

Having gotten here, I just want to remind you to please leave a review...an honest one.

Take just a few minutes of your time and leave me an honest review, the same way you will want guests to leave you their reviews. (Yes, I am trying to condition you.)

I want you to create your new Airbnb hosting account today.

Not tomorrow, today.

Thank you, again.

Kelly Higgins

Printed in Great Britain
by Amazon

53701701R00101